HOME GROWN GARDENING

# BEST PERENNIALS FOR SUN *and* SHADE

HOME GROWN GARDENING

# BEST PERENNIALS FOR SUN  SHADE

## EASY PLANTS FOR MORE BEAUTIFUL GARDENS

Houghton Mifflin Harcourt

BOSTON   NEW YORK   2019

Derived from *Taylor's 50 Best Perennials for Sun* and *Taylor's
50 Best Perennials for Shade*, produced by Storey Communications, Inc.
Copyright © 1999 by Houghton Mifflin Harcourt Publishing Company.

For information about permission to reproduce selections from this book,
write to trade.permissions@hmhco.com or to Permissions,
Houghton Mifflin Harcourt Publishing Company,
3 Park Avenue, 19th Floor, New York, New York 10016.

hmhco.com

Library of Congress Cataloging-in-Publication Data is available.
ISBN 978-1-328-62008-8

Printed in China
SCP 10 9 8 7 6 5 4 3 2 1

# CONTENTS

HOME GROWN GARDENING

# BEST PERENNIALS FOR SUN AND SHADE

# INTRODUCTION

Choosing perennials for your garden can be a daunting task, considering there are thousands of choices. To make the selection easier, this guide lists the easiest to grow and best-performing perennials for full sun and for partial and full shade. Each plant is shown in a color photo for easy identification. The photo is accompanied by information on where and how to grow the featured plant, along with horticultural tips to assist you in making your perennial gardening adventure an enjoyable and educational endeavor.

## what is a perennial?

Perennials are plants that persist year after year in a garden. They may be evergreen or deciduous, with the visible parts of the plants dying down each winter and new ones returning each spring from underground buds. Those perennials described as liking full sun need a location with no shade at all, or at least 8 hours with no shade. Perennials that require part shade require an area that receives 3 to 4 hours of direct sun each day in the early morning or evening, but not at midday. Planting on the east or west side of a building provides this type of shade. Part shade is also the filtered light provided by shade trees that have had their lower limbs removed to provide direct sunlight for short periods as the sun shines through gaps in the foliage. Full shade is shade provided by the north side of a building or from the cover of dense evergreen trees. It takes a special plant to thrive in these conditions.

## where to plant perennials

Most perennials make a stronger statement when planted in groups than if planted singly. Be careful about positioning plants together. Don't plant perennials that like dry soil next to ones that like wet soil, and avoid grouping plants with widely differing pH and fertilizer needs.

## SOIL PREPARATION

The key to successful gardening is adequate soil preparation. Unless you are blessed with good rich, deep loam, you will need to improve your garden soil to raise its fertility level and increase its organic content so that there is an ample supply of nutrients in a form that is readily available to plants. Soil for most perennials should be turned over with a shovel or spade to a depth of 10 to 12 inches.

Most perennials prefer soil that is slightly acidic (pH 6.5 to 6.8). To determine the pH of your soil, locate a soil-testing station in your area through the state Master Gardener program (home soil-testing kits are usually not very accurate). Follow the recommendations of the lab to adjust your soil's pH.

# FERTILIZING PLANTS

All plants need nutrients to maintain vigor. Some plants are heavy feeders and prefer frequent fertilizer applications; others are light feeders and only occasionally need supplementary feeding. Most perennials require a balanced fertilizer (the balance is between the three main ingredients—namely, nitrogen [N], phosphorus [P], and potassium [K]), as well as trace elements such as iron, boron, copper, zinc, and magnesium. As a general rule, plants grown for their foliage require a high-nitrogen fertilizer, a formula in which the first number is largest, such as 10-5-5. Plants grown for their flowers benefit from a higher phosphorus content (a formula such as 5-10-5). Organic fertilizers generally release nutrients more slowly but last longer than standard synthetic fertilizers. Calcium, another essential mineral, is usually added in the form of limestone. This also raises the pH; in areas where the pH is already high, use agricultural gypsum.

## mulching and winter protection

Mulch is a 2- to 4-inch layer of organic matter laid on the soil surface to retain moisture in the soil and to keep down weed growth. Preferred mulch materials include pine needles (white pine is best), shredded bark, shredded leaves, and bark chips. Mulch is best applied in fall as the plants are going dormant or in spring as plants start to grow.

In cold climates, apply a 6- to 10-inch layer of winter protection around the crowns of plants after the ground is frozen in early winter, and remove it when forsythia blooms in spring. It is especially important after fall planting to prevent unestablished plants from heaving out of the soil during alternating mild and cold spells.

## compost

Organic matter is vital to plants; it retains water in the soil and makes it available to plants, and it also provides food for bacteria that change nutrients into forms that can be absorbed by plants. Organic matter is decayed plant and animal remains; the best way to increase it is by adding well-aged compost (either purchased or homemade from garden debris or leaves), or well-aged horse or cow manure. (Poultry manure is usually too "hot" for most plants because it contains ammonia that may burn the leaves or roots.) Seaweed is another excellent source of organic matter, but it is not readily available to all gardeners.

## DRAINAGE

In soil that has a high sand or gravel content, many plants suffer from a lack of available water. The best way to increase the water-holding capacity of any soil is to increase its organic content. Conversely, wet soils need to be drained in order to increase the amount of oxygen that is available to plants. Soil drainage can be increased by adding organic matter (or very coarse sand, but organic matter is easier and supplies other benefits). For most perennials, water should never stand over their crowns for more than a few minutes after downpours—the exceptions are, of course, plants that naturally grow in wet spots. In very wet or heavy clay soils, where making the soil hospitable to plants is tough, it is usually easier to build raised beds on top of the soil using bricks, fieldstone, pressure-treated lumber (except near edible plants), or naturally rot-resistant wood such as red cedar or locust. Fill in the center with a mix of topsoil and compost.

# PLANTING PERENNIALS

Perennials are sold in two ways—as bare-root or container-grown plants. When planting a bare-root plant, dig a hole large enough so the roots can be spread out comfortably. Before planting, work a handful of a balanced fertilizer into the soil. Fill soil in around the roots and firm gently, making sure not to push down on the crown of the plant. Generally the crown of the plant (where the stem meets the roots) should be just below soil level.

When planting pot- or container-grown plants, be sure to tease the roots apart. If this is not done, the roots may girdle each other and choke off their food and water supply. It is also important to set the plant in the soil at the same level as it was in its container.

## controlling pests and diseases

Diagnosis is the key to pest and disease control. Ask for help from gardeners in the Master Gardener programs found in most states, or at your local Cooperative Extension Service; or look online or for a book on garden pests to help identify the problem and suggest preventive measures and possible cures. Use natural control methods wherever possible; avoid broad-spectrum pesticides—they are harmful to the user as well as the environment and they kill good predators along with pests.

# watering

Another key to successful gardening is watering. Provide too little water and plants perform poorly; too much and they're even worse. So how much is enough? First, all perennials should be well watered after planting. This settles the soil around the roots to establish good contact between the soil particles and newly developing root hairs. As a rule, during the growing season most perennials require 1 inch of water per week. Therefore, if it doesn't rain that amount, you will need to water them. Use a rain gauge situated in an open location to measure rain and irrigation. One sure way to "drown" perennials by overwatering is to put them on automatic timers that turn on irrigation water regardless of the amount of natural precipitation they receive.

How do you apply irrigation water? Soaker hoses are best for perennials; sprinklers have a tendency to weigh flowers down with water and splash mud on them, and encourage foliage diseases. A timer that turns the water on and off is a convenient way to use soaker hoses, taking care not to overwater during naturally wet periods.

## HARDINESS ZONES

Each plant listed in this guide has a hardiness rating. These numbers represent the cold and heat tolerance of the plants. Refer to the map on page 235 to determine your hardiness zone.

# BEST PERENNIALS FOR SUN

# YARROW

## how to grow

Grow yarrow in full sun for strong stems and rich flower colors. Aside from that, it's an undemanding plant and will grow well in any soil except a heavy, wet one. High on any list of drought-tolerant plants, yarrow is ideal for the spots your hose can't reach—or for parts of the country where water is scarce.

To propagate, divide plants in fall or early spring as soon as the first shoots appear. Dig up the plants and carefully pull them apart into three- to five-shoot clumps. Replant as quickly as you can at the same depth and water well.

Yarrow is such an easy-to-grow, decorative plant that new varieties are being introduced all the time. It has beautiful, fernlike green or gray-green leaves and masses of flowers that appear in flat clusters of tiny blossoms atop its strong stems. The flowers appear in a wide range of shades, including white, pale and hot pink, lavender, orange, peach, yellow, and red; they keep coming almost all summer.

## ACHILLEA

**ZONES:** 3–9

**BLOOM TIME:** Summer

**LIGHT:** Full sun

**HEIGHT:** 18–30 inches

**INTEREST:** Brightly colored blooms over a long season

## where to grow

Scatter groups of yarrow toward the middle to back of a mixed border—they don't care who their neighbors are; they look equally good with other perennials, as well as bulbs, shrubs, and annuals. Don't forget to plant some yarrow for cutting; it makes a wonderful addition to flower arrangements, both fresh and dried.

# AGASTACHE

## how to grow

Agastache is quite drought tolerant, though it does need well-drained, fertile soil. This is a fairly pest-free plant. It prefers full sun, though it will grow in part shade; it just won't flower as much.

With around 30 different species, Agastache comes in a variety of colors and is attractive to insects. Bluish purple flowers are most widespread, but others, such as this 'Peachie Keen', are worth searching out.

## where to grow

If you have a garden where rabbits or deer are troublesome, Agastache is a good choice, as they don't seem to like it.  Anywhere you want to attract hummingbirds and butterflies is also a good location. It is self-sowing, and you can transplant the seedlings; just be aware that the new plants may not be true to the parents.

### AGASTACHE
### AGASTACHE

**ZONES:** 4–10

**BLOOM TIME:** Summer

**LIGHT:** Full sun

**HEIGHT:** 2–4 feet

**INTEREST:** Aromatic, long-lasting flower spikes

# BLUE STAR

## how to grow

Blue star requires soil that doesn't dry out. Before planting, add organic matter (such as well-aged compost) to the soil. Mulch with 2 to 3 inches of pine needles or shredded bark to retain moisture.

Grown in part shade, the plants will grow new foliage if the flower stems are cut to about half their height after blossoms have faded. Stems bleed a milky sap when cut (see page 119). Plants rarely need dividing, but to increase your supply, divide into 4- to 6-inch clumps in spring before the brittle shoots start to emerge.

Blue star, also called willow amsonia, is a tidy plant with a long season of interest. In late spring, clusters of starry steel blue flowers appear atop 24- to 36-inch stems. Slender seedpods similar to those of milkweed but not as spectacular follow the blossoms. Then, at summer's end, the shiny, dark green willow-shaped leaves turn vivid yellow—guaranteed to brighten the dreariest fall day. This star performer requires little attention to keep it happy, although a nod of approval now and then won't go amiss.

## AMSONIA TABERNAE- MONTANA VAR. SALICIFOLIA

**ZONES:** 3–9

**BLOOM TIME:** Late spring

**LIGHT:** Full to part sun

**HEIGHT:** 24–36 inches

**INTEREST:** Clusters of steel blue star-shaped flowers; bright yellow foliage in autumn

## where to grow

Plant in full sun or part shade (advisable in the South). To fully appreciate the beauty of the flowers, give blue star a place at the front of a border. It is most attractive when placed in front of plants with bold foliage such as peonies, hostas, or oak-leaf hydrangeas. To enjoy the fall color to its fullest, plant blue star alongside plants with bronze or copper foliage.

# COLUMBINE

## how to grow

Columbine is easy to grow in average garden soil that is well drained. Plants tend to be short-lived, but since they grow readily from seeds, it's worth leaving some pods on the plants to ensure continuity. Be aware that the offspring are unlikely to be the same color as the parent, especially if there are other columbines nearby. If you wish to prevent self-sowing, deadhead the blossoms as soon as they fade. Columbine is sometimes attacked by an insect called a leaf miner that tunnels inside the leaves. To control this pest, remove and destroy the infested leaves; new leaves will grow to replace those you pluck off.

Columbines add a touch of elegance wherever they are grown. Native to North America, Europe, and Asia, they're delectable free-flowering plants that bloom in early summer in every color of the rainbow, in both single and double forms. Flowers of most species have attractive long tails, or spurs, protruding from the back. The delicate foliage is bright green in most varieties, bluish green in some. Columbine varieties cross-pollinate promiscuously, so plants routinely pop up in unexpected places and surprising colors.

## where to grow

Columbines never seem to look out of place. Plant them throughout the garden—in perennial and shrub borders, and in the rose garden to add variety of form and color. They are great self-hybridizers, so sprinkle seeds around and watch for new treasures to emerge in your garden.

## AQUILEGIA

**ZONES:** 3–9

**BLOOM TIME:** Late spring to early summer

**LIGHT:** Full to part sun

**HEIGHT:** 18–36 inches

**INTEREST:** Graceful flowers that dance gaily in the slightest breeze

# PERENNIAL DUSTY MILLER

## how to grow

Perennial dusty miller resents wet feet, so grow it in well-drained soil. It will thrive in ordinary soil as well as dry, sandy soil. In ideal conditions, it spreads readily and will smother its weaker neighbors; make sure they're strong enough to hold their own. Dusty miller's spreading habit makes it easy to produce new stock; just dig up the clumps in early spring, pull them apart into good-sized chunks, and replant them with the underground stems just below the surface of the soil. Though many people remove the flowers, it doesn't harm the plant to leave them on. Some flower arrangers find the spikes useful as fillers in small bouquets.

Also known as beach wormwood and old woman, perennial dusty miller is very hardy. The entire plant is densely clothed with feltlike silvery gray hairs that are very soft to the touch. Though dusty miller belongs to the daisy family, its yellowish flowers are not showy, and many gardeners remove them as they bloom. The plants have a spreading habit, growing three to four times as wide as their height of 1 to 2½ feet.

## ARTEMISIA STELLERANA

**ZONES:** 3–8

**BLOOM TIME:** Small, insignificant blooms in summer

**LIGHT:** Full sun

**HEIGHT:** 12–30 inches

**INTEREST:** Densely felted gray foliage

## where to grow

This plant can be grown in a rock garden or at the front edge of a border with low-growing perennials, annuals, or dwarf shrubs. It can also be underplanted with miniature bulbs, such as crocuses, dwarf irises, and dwarf daffodils, or it can act as a ground cover for a dry, sandy bank. Combine perennial dusty miller with other dwarf plants to line a path or use in window boxes. It is unsuitable for the Deep South—in hot, humid climates, replace perennial dusty miller with the annual dusty miller, *Senecio cineraria;* it behaves like a perennial in mild climates.

# BUTTERFLY WEED

## how to grow

Butterfly weed must be grown in full sun with good drainage. It thrives in light, sandy soils—in fact, it flourishes in the almost pure sand of Martha's Vineyard, one of the many areas where it is native. Propagation is tricky and is best left to a professional. It is not advisable to move plants once they are established (do not transplant them from the wild); the brittle roots snap off easily, causing an almost always fatal shock.

Butterfly weed, a milkweed, is one of eastern North America's most brightly colored wildflowers. In summer, plants are topped with dense clusters of curiously shaped blossoms. New cultivars come in a variety of colors, while the wildflower is almost always orange. When using it for cut flowers, flame the stems to stop the flow of milky sap (see page 119). Butterfly weed's spectacular flowers are followed in early fall by seedpods that burst, releasing their feathered seeds to float like dancing angels on the breeze.

## where to grow

Plant these hot-colored plants with other vibrant bloomers to create a garden sensation. Alternatively, group with plants with white flowers and those with gray foliage, to shine as the stars of the show. Combined with yarrows, coneflowers, sedums, and many ornamental grasses, butterfly weed can turn a dry or sandy slope into a stunning summer flower garden.

### ASCLEPIAS TUBEROSA

**ZONES:** 3–9

**BLOOM TIME:** Summer

**LIGHT:** Full sun

**HEIGHT:** 12–24 inches

**INTEREST:** Blooms in vibrant shades of yellow, orange, and red; makes long-lasting cut flowers; irresistible to butterflies, particularly monarchs

# FRIKART'S ASTER

## how to grow

Frikart's aster grows well in ordinary garden soil where it can get lots of water in the summer, but where water does not stand in winter. Deadheading encourages more abundant flowering. In the North, protect it over winter with a layer of evergreen branches to shade the soil and keep it at a more uniform temperature. Do not use mulch over the crowns (at any time of the year), as this can hold dampness that may cause plants to rot. In the Deep South, Frikart's aster is best treated as an annual. Take stem cuttings in summer to propagate.

This Swiss-bred hybrid ranks among the world's great garden plants—many noted horticulturists insist it belongs in every garden. Such praise is understandable. This aster blends well with just about every other flower color and looks as good in a vase as it does in the garden. The plants have graceful 24- to 36-inch stems, and they're little bothered by pests.

## ASTER X FRIKARTII

**ZONES:** 5–8

**BLOOM TIME:** Summer

**LIGHT:** Full sun; flowers poorly in shade

**HEIGHT:** 24–36 inches

**INTEREST:** Abundant blue daisies over a long period

## where to grow

Plant Frikart's aster in the front portion of a sunny perennial border, where it blends with most other plants and will provide abundant color for months. It can also look striking in a large rock garden planted in front of a boulder or dark conifer. Its continuous flowering habit makes this an ideal plant for growing in a container on a sunny patio or deck, either on its own or with other long-blooming plants.

# FALSE INDIGO

## how to grow

This plant is practically indestructible—it will remain vigorous long after the gardener has thrown in the trowel. In fact, once it is well established you almost need a backhoe to move it; with this in mind, plant false indigo in well-drained soil in a spot where you want it to stay. In full sun, false indigo blooms profusely and needs no staking.

It will do almost as well in 3 to 4 hours of light shade, with bloom only slightly diminished, though plants may require staking. Start new plants from seeds. If you allow the seeds to ripen and fall, you may find seedlings close to the base of the parent plants; keep your eyes open for telltale gray-green leaves.

False indigo has brilliant blue, pealike blossoms on 10- to 12-inch flower spikes that appear around the time peonies bloom. Flowers are followed by attractive seedpods that start out green but gradually turn black and persist until fall. The grayish green foliage has a cool, pleasant, shrublike appearance and remains appealing until frost cuts it down. Its long-lasting foliage makes false indigo a useful background for plants that are later blooming.

## where to grow

Shrublike false indigo makes its presence known in any mixed border. It can be surprisingly effective as a seasonal hedge or foundation planting, serving the visual function of a shrub in three seasons and disappearing in winter. Try it where ice sliding off a roof prevents you from growing shrubs.

## BAPTISIA AUSTRALIS

**ZONES:** 3–9

**BLOOM TIME:** Midspring to early summer

**LIGHT:** Full or part sun (tolerates 3 to 4 hours of light shade each day)

**HEIGHT:** 36–48 inches

**INTEREST:** Brilliant blue flowers; attractive gray-green foliage; black seedpods

# BOLTONIA

## how to grow

This extremely low-maintenance plant will grow just about anywhere it receives full sun. It tolerates damp or dry soil, but it prefers rich soil liberally amended with organic matter. Cut the plants down in late fall after hard frost. Increase the number of plants by dividing the crowns in early spring before new shoots appear. Boltonia is pest- and disease-free.

Easy-to-grow boltonia has willowlike grayish green foliage on stiffly erect plants that are smothered with white or pink daisies from August to early October. Boltonia is useful as a vertical accent or planted in a large group to provide a strong architectural presence. Backed by sugar maples in their full fall color, this 3- to 5-foot mass of flowers makes a memorable sight. The variety *latisquama* is shown here.

## BOLTONIA ASTEROIDES

**ZONES:** 4–8

**BLOOM TIME:** Late summer to early fall

**LIGHT:** Full sun in the North; light, midday shade in the South

**HEIGHT:** 36–60 inches

**INTEREST:** Masses of white asterlike flowers

## where to grow

For the best effect, grow boltonia in full sun surrounded by low-growing plants that won't block the light from its base—allowing it to bloom all the way down. Plant it with shrubs that offer good fall color and grasses that bloom at that time. Its stately presence in a bed with low-growing annuals provides contrast and will take over the main show when the annuals start to look tired in late summer. Boltonia also makes a superb hedge for summer and dies down in winter.

# FEATHER REED GRASS

## how to grow

Does best in rich, moist soil but can adapt to dry soils as well, and thrives in clay soil. Prune close to the ground in early spring. Divide in late winter to early spring, every three years or so. Very resistant to pests and diseases.

'Karl Foerster' is a cultivar of feather reed grass that has become very popular—and no wonder, with its dramatic feathery plumes.

## where to grow

Its upright, vertical habit makes it useful as a border accent, as a backdrop for smaller plants. It is also a good choice to combine with late bloomers, as a counterpart to fall colors.

### CALAMAGROSTIS X ACUTIFLORA

**ZONES:** 4–9

**BLOOM TIME:** Summer

**LIGHT:** Full to part sun

**HEIGHT:** 3–5 feet

**INTEREST:** Feathery flower stalks in summer, golden seed heads fall into winter

# CALAMINT

## how to grow

Like all mints, calamint is easy to grow, but unlike true mints (*Mentha* species), it is a tidy, well-behaved plant that is not determined to take over the world. Plant it in full sun in ordinary soil. Calamint is drought tolerant, so it fares well in light, sandy soil. The only maintenance required is cutting the wiry stems close to the ground in late winter or early spring before new shoots appear. Calamint is pest-free; it can be divided in early spring to provide new plants. Cuttings root easily.

Calamint (sometimes called beautiful mint) is a charming Old World species with tiny, sparkling blossoms in late summer and continuing into mid-autumn. It shrugs off light frost and provides a cheerful sight after most plants have given up for the year and there is little color left in the garden. Another delightful feature of this plant is the pungent aroma that fills the air when the foliage is brushed. This treat can be enjoyed throughout the year, even after calamint has succumbed to frost—but be sure to wait until late winter or early spring before cutting it back.

## CALAMINTHA NEPETA

**ZONES:** 5–9

**BLOOM TIME:** Late summer to fall

**LIGHT:** Full sun

**HEIGHT:** 12–24 inches

**INTEREST:** Clouds of tiny light blue and white flowers surrounded by foliage

## where to grow

Grow calamint in a location you pass frequently to enjoy its fragrance and exquisite little flowers. Next to the kitchen door is ideal. In foundation plantings, calamint adds sparkle. Try it, too, at the front of a border or alongside shrubs such as roses. It's also perfect in a narrow border by itself, underplanted with bulbs. Don't forget to add this plant to an herb or vegetable garden and use it as a cut flower in mixed arrangements. It complements hot and cool colors, so don't worry about where to plant it in relationship to the other flowers in your garden.

# CARPATHIAN BELLFLOWER

## how to grow

Carpathian bellflower grows best in the cooler parts of the country; it does poorly in hot, humid environments. Provide full sun or part shade (especially in warmer regions) and good drainage to keep bellflower content. Deadheading encourages repeat bloom and discourages an overabundance of self-sown seedlings (leave a few seedpods on the plant if you want a few more plants). Slugs are the only enemy; reduce damage from these critters by following the directions on page 118.

Carpathian bellflower is one of the most handsome low-growing plants for the front of the border. In midsummer, it produces masses of brilliant blue flowers that are shaped like little bells (*Campanula* means "little bell" in Latin) and nod slightly on 8-inch stems. The plants spread slowly. When this plant is in bloom, the foliage can hardly be seen because there are so many flowers. This bellflower is easy to grow and adds bright, reliable color to the summer garden.

## where to grow

Carpathian bellflower belongs at the front of every perennial border, where its brilliant splash of blue can be best appreciated. It is also suited for growing in rock gardens and along the tops of rock walls, where it can spill down to make a colorful, cascading show. Carpathian bellflower fares well in containers such as window boxes and patio planters, provided that the plants are not kept too wet or allowed to dry out too much.

### CAMPANULA CARPATICA

**ZONES:** 3–8

**BLOOM TIME:** Midsummer

**LIGHT:** Full to part sun

**HEIGHT:** 8 inches

**INTEREST:** Masses of brilliant blue bell-shaped flowers on a low, spreading plant that makes a great ground cover

# BLUE-MIST SHRUB

## how to grow

In Zones 5 and 6, stems are likely to be damaged by winter, so it's best to prune the plant back to the ground in the spring. Because it blooms on new growth, it will still flower well (so even in warmer zones pruning will help promote robust growth). It is drought tolerant and prefers well-drained soil.

*Caryopteris x clandonensis* has beautiful purple-blue blossoms from late summer through the first heavy winter frost. It is also known as bluebeard and blue spirea.

## CARYOPTERIS

**ZONES:** 5–9

**BLOOM TIME:** Late summer into fall

**LIGHT:** Full sun

**HEIGHT:** 2–3 feet

**INTEREST:** Bluish to purple flowers and fragrant foliage

## where to grow

Deer are not interested in blue-mist shrub, but butterflies, bees, and other pollinators are. It works well in borders and as a hedge and is of particular use in fall, when little else is blooming.

# PERENNIAL CORNFLOWER

## how to grow

Plant perennial cornflower and stand back. No, it's not that bad! It grows in almost any soil, but it flops over if allowed to dry out too much. It is more aggressive in rich soils, so avoid fertilizing. Deadhead as soon as flowers are spent to keep it blossoming and reduce the number of self-sown seedlings. Like all spreaders, it is easily increased by dividing the clumps or by transplanting the seedlings. Perennial cornflower does best in cool regions and does not like hot, humid climates.

Also called mountain bluet, perennial cornflower is a European member of the vast daisy family. Its brilliant deep blue blossoms, 2 to 3 inches across, are touched with red at the center. The uniquely shaped petals are frilled and fringed in a delicate arrangement on a thistlelike flower head. Perennial cornflower provides an ample supply of cut flowers that enrich any flower arrangement. (Annual cornflower is also called bachelor's button and is one of the most useful flowers in the cutting garden.)

## where to grow

Perennial cornflower thrives in full sun but is almost as happy in part shade, where it has a tendency to be floppier. Since this plant can be a spreader (especially in northern gardens), locate it with care. Avoid placing perennial cornflower in a border with delicate plants that are easily overcome by aggressive colonizers. Take advantage of cornflower's habit by using it to hold a sunny bank, but be careful not to let the soil dry out before the cornflower is well established. It provides a colorful companion for all but the shortest of shrubs.

### CENTAUREA MONTANA

**ZONES:** 3–8

**BLOOM TIME:** Summer

**LIGHT:** Full to part sun

**HEIGHT:** 18–24 inches

**INTEREST:** Masses of frilly brilliant blue flowers over a long season

# RED VALERIAN

## how to grow

Red valerian, a Mediterranean native, fares best in well-drained soil in full sun. It tolerates drought but not shade—there its growth is poor and it doesn't flower well. Plant red valerian in spring from container-grown specimens. Plants respond to cutting by producing more flowers, making this an excellent choice for the cutting garden. Deadhead frequently to encourage more blossoms and to prevent unwanted seedlings of different hues than the parent plant. Propagate from seeds in early spring in a heated greenhouse or simply buy starter plants from your local nursery.

Red valerian is a fine border plant with clusters of red, deep pink, rose-pink, or pure white, lightly fragrant flowers that top willowlike gray-green leaves. It starts flowering in late spring and repeats all summer and into fall, even sporadically through the winter in California, especially if spent flowers are removed promptly. Red valerian adds a colorful note to a vase of cut flowers.

## CENTRANTHUS RUBER

**ZONES:** 5–8

**BLOOM TIME:** Early summer to late fall

**LIGHT:** Full sun

**HEIGHT:** 36 inches

**INTEREST:** Showy red, pink, or white, lightly fragrant flowers; attractive grayish green leaves

## where to grow

Plant red valerian in a sunny border next to white- or blue-flowered plants such as delphiniums and columbines, with gray-foliaged artemisias, or in front of shrubs with purple or bronze foliage such as smoke tree or weigela. This plant is equally at home in the Northeast and the Northwest, but not in the Deep South, where hot, muggy nights take their toll.

# THREAD-LEAVED COREOPSIS

## how to grow

Thread-leaved coreopsis is very easy to grow. It is drought tolerant and grows well in sandy soils, but it fares less well in heavy, wet ones. Feed with a low-nitrogen plant food immediately after the first flush of flowers has been cut back. Divide after 2 to 3 years. Propagate by rooting summer cuttings taken from nonflowering stems (see page 118).

Thread-leaved coreopsis is noted for its yellow (but sometimes pink) flowers that appear in prodigious quantities all summer. It is indispensable in the garden and looks its best planted in sweeps of ten or more (you simply can't have too many). Its colors blend well with every other color in the rainbow, and the foliage is neat and tidy. Thread-leaved coreopsis is a thoroughly well-behaved perennial, deserving of a reputation as one of the world's great garden plants. It has one minor flaw: a tendency to spread a little too freely in climates that remain warm and moist all summer.

## where to grow

Without qualification, thread-leaved coreopsis belongs in every perennial bed or mixed border; it is that good. It adds lots of color to plantings of ornamental grasses, especially those that give their main show in fall when they blossom. Although it blooms most heavily in full sun, in the South coreopsis needs light shade. It's also useful as a ground cover since its dense habit will choke out all but the most persistent of weeds. Coreopsis adds consistent color to shrub plantings, most of which bloom in spring. It's nearly impossible to plant it with a color with which it clashes.

### COREOPSIS VERTICILLATA

**ZONES:** 3–9

**BLOOM TIME:** Midsummer until frost

**LIGHT:** Full sun in the North; light shade in the South

**HEIGHT:** 24–36 inches

**INTEREST:** Lacy green foliage topped with myriad bright yellow flowers

# DELPHINIUM

## how to grow

Delphiniums require soil that retains moisture but never becomes waterlogged (especially in winter). They are heavy feeders, succeeding best where the soil is deeply cultivated with lots of added organic matter. Apply a low-nitrogen fertilizer liberally in early spring. Staking is essential (see page 115. Cut the spikes back to the top of the foliage after blossoming for repeat blooms in late summer and early fall.

Delphinium is one of the great plants of Europe. The *belladonna* types grow 4 to 5 feet tall and are the most durable varieties available (lasting 3 to 4 years) for American gardeners. They come in an assortment of blue, purple, and white shades but lack the grandeur of the more stately delphiniums of European gardens. The *elatum* hybrids, while long-lasting perennials in Europe, perform brilliantly in American gardens for just a year or two. This makes them magnificent, if somewhat expensive, annuals or biennials. They're worth trying, though, especially in northern and coastal gardens. ('Magic Fountains' is shown here.)

## DELPHINIUM

**ZONES:** 3–8

**BLOOM TIME:** Summer

**LIGHT:** Full sun

**HEIGHT:** 48–60 inches

**INTEREST:** Light blue spikes on tall plants

## where to grow

Delphiniums must have full sun and should be planted at the back of the perennial border. They resent the heat and humidity of the Southeast, succeeding best where nights cool down. They are magnificent as cut flowers, providing height, color, and drama in mixed bouquets.

# GARDEN PINK

## how to grow

All garden pinks are not too fussy about soil conditions, but they do require good drainage. They will grow with abandon in any reasonable garden soil. Deadheading (see page 117) encourages even more blossoms. Because this, like other garden pinks, prefers a pH close to neutral, give it a yearly handful of ground dolomitic limestone everywhere but in alkaline regions of the country.

There are more than 300 species of Dianthus, and thousands of cultivars. Carnations are in the same family. The bright pink hybrid 'Kahori' is shown here. It blooms from late spring to early summer.

## where to grow

This adaptable plant will tolerate a wide variety of growing conditions, so it allows many options for garden placement. It is equally at home at the edge of a garden border, along paths, in pockets in a dry stone wall, in rock gardens, on dry sunny banks, and in containers.

### DIANTHUS

**ZONES:** 4–8

**BLOOM TIME:** Summer

**LIGHT:** Full sun

**HEIGHT:** 8–10 inches

**INTEREST:** Masses of fragrant, fringed single pink blossoms that appear in early summer

# PERENNIAL FOXGLOVE

## how to grow

Foxglove requires moist (not wet) soils and resents drying out. To ensure these conditions, apply liberal quantities of organic matter to the soil before planting and again in spring before plants are in active growth. The only maintenance required is to remove the dead flower spikes. Do this as the flowers are spent and before the plants put energy into seed production. Remember to leave a few seedpods if you want more plants.

Perennial foxglove (also known by the botanical name *Digitalis grandiflora*) is one of the few truly perennial foxgloves. Most other foxgloves are biennial—they produce leaves one year, flower the next, produce seeds, then die. Perennial foxglove, on the other hand, lasts in the garden for years. In mild climates, its foliage is evergreen. The pale yellow spikes blend well with almost every other shade, so it's easy to combine it with other plants. Like its shorter-lived relatives, it makes an excellent cut flower; for best results, cut stems when about half their buds have opened.

### DIGITALIS GRANDIFLORA

**ZONES:** 4–8

**BLOOM TIME:** Early summer, with repeat bloom until fall

**LIGHT:** Full to part sun

**HEIGHT:** 30–36 inches

**INTEREST:** Pale yellow flowers

## where to grow

Perennial foxglove is a versatile plant that tolerates both full sun and part shade. The pale yellow flowers look best when planted next to hot-colored flowers; they manage to get your attention without making a scene. Perennial foxglove is equally at home in a formal perennial garden, mixed border, or naturalized woodland setting.

# CONEFLOWER

## how to grow

Coneflowers grow well in average garden soils and in hot, dry conditions, but they resent wet feet. They are equally happy in either full or part sun and require only deadheading to keep them blooming vigorously and to keep them tidy. They will self-sow, with seedlings usually varying in shade from the parent plant but attractive nonetheless. The plants never require staking, but they are prey to Japanese beetles. (See page 116 for ways to control this pest.) In the South, divide the plant crowns every 3 to 4 years to keep coneflowers vigorous.

This North American native, closely related to black-eyed Susan, is a must for the perennial border. A great garden plant, coneflower has brightly colored blossoms in shades of purplish red, rosy pink, carmine, or crimson-red—depending on how you see color. (*Echinacea purpurea*, purple coneflower, is shown here.) Pure white selections provide an interesting contrast when planted with the brighter shades. Flowers start blooming in June above dark green foliage and continue until frost. All summer, clouds of butterflies find the blossoms irresistible. Coneflowers are a wonderful addition to summer bouquets; after the petals have fallen, the cones are a nice addition to dried arrangements.

## where to grow

Coneflowers belong in every perennial border and cutting garden, in meadows, or planted alongside liatris and butterfly bush in a garden for butterflies and summer color. The brightly colored flowers and the butterflies they attract make them great plants for children to grow.

### ECHINACEA

**ZONES:** 4–9

**BLOOM TIME:** June to frost

**LIGHT:** Full to part sun

**HEIGHT:** 24–40 inches

**INTEREST:** Very large rose, pink, or white daisies; butterflies love them

# GLOBE THISTLE

## how to grow

Globe thistle prefers full sun and average to rich well-drained garden soil. It is very drought tolerant and can thrive in conditions that would wilt other perennials. Taller varieties need staking in windy locations and excessively fertile soil. They are very long-lasting, low-maintenance plants. Propagate from seeds, or root cuttings, or by division.

Globe thistle, with its prickly personality, will never gain stardom in the border, but this European native does provide a steel blue color and round shape found in no other flower. It is excellent for fresh flower arrangements and very enticing to honeybees and moths. The attractive foliage is not as daunting as the plant's common name would suggest— globe is not a true thistle, just a good imitator. It is a tough, no-nonsense perennial that grows almost anywhere. 'Veitch's Blue' is shown here.

## ECHINOPS RITRO

**ZONES:** 3–10

**BLOOM TIME:** Mid- to late summer

**LIGHT:** Full sun

**HEIGHT:** 2–4 feet

**INTEREST:** Unique round steel blue flower heads; dramatic foliage

## where to grow

Plant globe thistle at the back or in the middle of a mixed border, where its unusual color and flower shape will provide an interesting contrast to other perennials. Globe thistle is also useful in meadow gardens, where it will thrive for years with little or no attention. Plant it in front of tall grasses for a backdrop for its unusual flowers, or combine it with other summer bloomers such as day lilies, purple coneflower, bee balm, and phlox.

# SEA HOLLY

## how to grow

Sea holly is easy to grow in full sun and is tolerant of most soils except wet ones. Staking and deadheading are never needed, so this plant is really low maintenance and is almost pest-free. Dividing sea holly is somewhat tricky because of its taproot; divide in spring for best results. It is easiest to propagate plants from root cuttings (see page 115).

Sea holly is a uniquely beautiful ornamental plant with blossoms, bracts, and stems a striking shade of amethyst blue. It produces teasel-like flowers in prodigious quantities. The flowers are long lasting in fresh bouquets and fine in dried arrangements. There is much confusion about the names of the various sea hollies, as they are somewhat promiscuous, but all the progeny are attractive and should not be ignored simply because they lack a pedigree. Plants propagated vegetatively (by root cuttings) are identical to the parent. Seed-grown plants may not be.

## where to grow

In spite of its name, sea holly prefers locations with average to dry soil, in full sun. It tolerates drought and shrugs off saltwater spray, making it ideal for coastal gardens.

### ERYNGIUM AMETHYSTINUM

**ZONES:** 5–10

**BLOOM TIME:** Midsummer

**LIGHT:** Full sun

**HEIGHT:** 36 inches

**INTEREST:** Masses of teasel-like flowers in amethyst blue that are lovely fresh or dried

# SPURGE

## how to grow

To encourage new growth, cut back by about one-third after the plant is done flowering for the season. (Though see below about the toxic sap.) Most spurges are quite drought tolerant, and most love sun, but some types do well in shade.

There are more than 2,000 kinds of these tough, easy-to-grow plants. Some euphorbias love sun, while others love shade; some are drought tolerant, and others prefer more moisture. *Euphorbia polychroma* (shown here) is known as cushion spurge for its dome-shaped growing habit.

## EUPHORBIA

**ZONES:** 4–10

**BLOOM TIME:** Spring to summer

**LIGHT:** Full sun to partial shade

**HEIGHT:** 6 inches to 3 feet

**INTEREST:** Colorful leaves and interesting flowers

## where to grow

The milky white sap is a deterrent to deer and other pests (and it can be irritating to skin, so wear gloves and wash immediately if you come in contact with it). Spurges are an excellent inclusion in rock gardens.

# SWEET JOE-PYE WEED

## how to grow

With sturdy stems with whorls of pink flowers in midsummer, sweet Joe-Pye weed does well in full sun but can tolerate shade and prefers moist soil but tolerates dry soil. A low-maintenance choice, it is also resistant to pests.

Native to the East Coast of North America, sweet Joe-Pye weed attracts bees, moths, and butterflies. The showy, domed mauve-pink flower clusters are followed by seed heads that last into winter. 'Gateway' is shown here.

## where to grow

Deer resistant and attractive to butterflies and other pollinators, sweet Joe-Pye weed works well planted in masses at the back of a border in moist, fertile soil. It can also provide erosion control in sites that need it.

### EUTROCHIUM PURPUREUM

**ZONES:** 4–9

**BLOOM TIME:** Mid- to late summer

**LIGHT:** Full sun to partial shade

**HEIGHT:** 5–6 feet

**INTEREST:** Vanilla-scented pale pink flowers

# BLANKET FLOWER

## how to grow

Blanket flower requires full sun and a light, well-drained soil that is low in nutrients. Avoid fertilizers, or the plants will produce lush foliage that is more susceptible to rot. Deadheading, a necessary chore for most plants, is usually not needed to keep the plants blooming. Blanket flower tends to be short-lived in the garden, especially in the South. It is easy to propagate by division or from seeds, and starter plants are relatively inexpensive at garden centers.

When other plants buckle under to heat and humidity, blanket flower continues to shine—even in the South, where other plants take a siesta when the temperatures rise. North or South, this plant is easy to grow and produces lots of brightly colored flowers that last a long time in both garden and vase. The blossoms can be single or semidouble and appear in shades of yellow and red, or in bands of both on the same flower.

## GAILLARDIA X GRANDIFLORA

**ZONES:** Zones 3–10

**BLOOM TIME:** Summer into fall

**LIGHT:** Full sun

**HEIGHT:** 24–36 inches

**INTEREST:** Masses of brightly colored daisylike flowers

## where to grow

Blanket flower is as versatile as it is colorful. Given a prominent spot in the perennial border, this vibrant gem will produce an eye-catching display all summer long. Its proclivity for blooming also makes it an invaluable plant in dry meadows. Plant enough to use for floral arrangements, too. You'll find blanket flower used extensively in wildflower seed mixtures for naturalizing.

# PERENNIAL GERANIUM

## how to grow

Perennial geranium is generally easy to grow and thrives in ordinary, well-drained, fertile soil. In the North it prefers full sun, but in the heat and humidity of the South it requires protection from afternoon sun. (High shade from trees is ideal.) It is virtually pest- and disease-free, which is always a blessing. If the plants become straggly after flowering, as they often do in part shade, cut them back to the new foliage.

Perennial geranium, also known as cranesbill, has a strong personality for a small plant, perhaps the reason for its reputation as a must-have plant for gardeners everywhere. When in bloom, it virtually covers itself with striking blue or pink flowers. The blooms are set off with pleasing, deeply divided bright green leaves. (The hybrid Rozanne is shown here.) *NOTE:* Perennial geraniums are not to be confused with *Pelargonium*—the ubiquitous pot geranium with spheres of brilliant red or pink flowers.

## where to grow

Place perennial geranium in a prominent location at the front of a border, surrounded by more subtle shades that complement its showoff personality. It can also be used as a ground cover between shrubs such as bridalwreath spirea, but allow plenty of space between the shrubs so the geraniums are not heavily shaded.

### GERANIUM

**ZONES:** 4–7

**BLOOM TIME:** Early summer to fall

**LIGHT:** Full sun to light shade

**HEIGHT:** 15–18 inches

**INTEREST:** Masses of pink or blue blossoms; attractive lacy leaves

# SNEEZEWEED

## how to grow

Sneezeweed prefers full sun in evenly moist soil but will tolerate wet areas. If your soil tends to dry out, water often and add lots of organic matter such as leaf mold or well-rotted compost to retain moisture. Taller varieties require staking unless you cut the stems back to half their height in late June. The shorter plants will grow bushier and produce even more flowers. To propagate, divide plants in early spring just as the new shoots appear.

Sneezeweed is a valuable addition to the mixed border because its bloom time comes after most perennials have given up for the year. The flowers, in glowing autumn shades of yellow, red, and bronze, appear on strong, stiffly upright stems and are ideal for cutting. They also provide food for butterflies on their southerly migration. Despite its common name, sneezeweed does not cause sneezing. Hybridizers have combined the hardiness of this eastern species with the larger, brighter-colored flowers of western species to produce many vividly colored selections, such as 'Mardi Gras', shown here.

### HELENIUM AUTUMNALE

**ZONES:** 3–10

**BLOOM TIME:** Late summer to early fall

**LIGHT:** Full sun

**HEIGHT:** 48–60 inches

**INTEREST:** Masses of autumn-colored flowers

## where to grow

Plant sneezeweed toward the middle or back of a mixed border. It is especially useful for filling in after spring-flowering perennials, such as bleeding heart, have declined. Sneezeweed is an excellent cut flower, providing abundant color in floral arrangements.

# PERENNIAL SUNFLOWER

## how to grow

Perennial sunflower does best in regularly fertilized soil (spring and fall) amended with organic matter, such as rotted manure. After flowering is complete, cut plants back to the ground. It likes soil that doesn't dry out too much in summer; water during rainless spells. In the North and West this sunflower prefers full sun; in the South it appreciates some shade, though if it's too dark stems will need staking. Pinch growing tips in mid-June (late May in the South) to increase branching and reduce the need for staking.

Bushy, bright green foliage makes a perfect foil for the masses of golden yellow blossoms characteristic of the showy perennial sunflower. This bold plant adds a clear, cheery note to any border or vase. Perennial sunflower is a very tall hybrid that is well mannered in the border, growing vigorously but not invasively. Its relatives include the much-loved and useful annual sunflower (*Helianthus annuus*) and Jerusalem artichoke (*H. tuberosus*), which is a confusing colloquial name for this North American sunflower.

## where to grow

Perennial sunflower is a big plant that needs ample room to grow. Group several at the back of a mixed shrub and perennial border, or use as a screen to block an unsightly view or provide privacy during summer. A group of three or more is also ideal located in the center of a large island bed.

### HELIANTHUS X MULTIFLORUS

**ZONES:** 4–10

**BLOOM TIME:** Mid- to late summer

**LIGHT:** Full sun (part shade in the South)

**HEIGHT:** 48–60 inches

**INTEREST:** Lots of long-lasting blooms

# FALSE SUNFLOWER

## how to grow

False sunflower tolerates drier soils than perennial sunflower and requires little in the way of fertilizing. Plants require staking unless they're cut back to half their height in mid-June. Regular deadheading increases the number of blooms and decreases the number of volunteer seedlings. The only other required care is to cut the plants to the ground after frost has ended their blooming season.

This North American native perennial closely resembles perennial sunflower and produces a fine show of 3- to 4-inch yellow or yellowish orange daisies for most of the summer. The blossoms of false sunflower are either single, semidouble (with petals surrounding the dark centers), or fully double (completely concealing the center). This plant has found a well-deserved home in perennial borders around the world because it is so free flowering and trouble-free. As a cut flower, it is long lasting and always perky. 'Summer Sun' is shown here.

**HELIOPSIS HELIANTHOIDES**

**ZONES:** 4–9

**BLOOM TIME:** Midsummer to fall

**LIGHT:** Full sun

**HEIGHT:** 48–60 Inches

**INTEREST:** Prolific, relatively large golden or yellow blossoms

## where to grow

False sunflower is a tidy, well-behaved plant that fits into any perennial or mixed border. It can be used as a specimen plant among shorter perennials or amid taller neighbors such as ornamental grasses or shrubs. It is superb when cut for use in summer and fall floral arrangements.

# DAYLILY

## how to grow

Daylilies tolerate even poor soil as long as it's well drained, but they grow best in good, rich, deeply worked soil. Mulch well and water during rainless spells to ensure flower production throughout dry times. Fertilize in early spring and late fall. One regular chore remains. Remove each day's spent blossoms to keep plants looking tidy. Each one lasts only a day, hence the Latin name *Hemerocallis*, meaning "beautiful for a day." Divide in spring or fall if flowering declines.

Daylilies are as tough as iron; they spread quickly but not aggressively and flower freely. They're not very fussy about growing conditions. Thanks to enthusiastic hybridizers, there are more than thirty thousand varieties in every color, such as this 'Red Razzmatazz'. Daylilies are often confused with true lilies, which grow from bulbs and have leaves that clothe the flower stem. In contrast, daylilies have fleshy roots and coarse, grasslike foliage that grows directly from the crown of the plant.

## where to grow

Horticulturists consider the daylily one of the backbone plants of a border. Its habit of flowering over a long period makes it invaluable massed in a bed or for use in a mixed planting with other perennials, shrubs, or both. Daylilies make a great ground cover, as their vigorous growth chokes out most weeds. Use them on sunny banks, where their strong roots help hold the soil in place. They can also be naturalized along roadsides and in wild gardens.

## HEMEROCALLIS

**ZONES:** 3–9

**BLOOM TIME:** Summer

**LIGHT:** Full sun

**HEIGHT:** 24–48 inches

**INTEREST:** Brilliant blossoms in myriad hues on tidy, easy-care plants

# JAPANESE IRIS

## how to grow

Japanese iris has three essential requirements: sun, acidic soil, and abundant moisture. It requires no other care beyond picking off Japanese beetles, which have a fondness for the flowers (see page 116). Divide in late August to give the plants a chance to become well established before winter. Protection is necessary for the first winter in northern climates (see page 117).

When it's in bloom, Japanese iris provides one of the most outstanding floral displays a garden can feature. For hundreds of years, specialists in Japan have been hybridizing this plant to produce some of the largest flowers of any perennial (up to 10 inches across), in shades of lavender, maroon, mauve, pink, purple, and white. One of the delights of Japanese iris is that all the subtle variations in hue are perfectly complementary to each other. The long, swordlike foliage remains attractive even after the flowers fade. This *kaempferi* is a variegated form.

### IRIS ENSATA

**ZONES:** 4–9

**BLOOM TIME:** Midsummer

**LIGHT:** Full sun

**HEIGHT:** 24–48 inches

**INTEREST:** Huge orchid-like blossoms that float like exotic birds above rich green foliage

## where to grow

Japanese irises thrive in wet soils, so they're ideal for the edges of ponds and streams. Plant as a delicate accent in a mixed border or in groups by themselves— in a location where you can bask in the full impact of their delightful beauty. Since Japanese irises make astonishing cut flowers, be sure to make room for them in a wet corner of the cutting garden.

# BEARDED IRIS

## how to grow

Bearded irises prefer full sun, though in warmer regions they like some light shade. Grow these beauties in loose, fertile soil that has been amended with organic matter. Proper planting is very important. Plant iris rhizomes in well-drained soil in late summer. (1) Dig a hole large enough to accommodate all roots; form a ridge of soil in the bottom. (2) Spread roots out over the ridge. Add more soil as needed until rhizomes sit horizontal to the soil level. Cover with ½ inch of soil. (3) Divide the roots every 3 to 4 years to keep plants vigorous.

Iris borer is a major pest that tunnels into the thick rhizome. If you see spots like water streaks on leaves, feel the rhizome tops for soft spots; dig up any suspicious rhizomes to look for (and destroy) white borers inside. To reduce susceptibility, space plants 12 to 18 inches apart for best air circulation, and do not mulch.

Bearded irises provide flamboyance to any garden because they come in dwarf, intermediate, and tall sizes. The brilliant colors of the blossoms are often unique to the world of flowers and were created by complicated hybridization. Some people consider bearded irises untidy looking after the flowers fade, so they prefer to grow these delicious beauties in an area by themselves, or in a location where the swordlike leaves will be hidden by neighboring plants.

## where to grow

Bearded irises are available in tall (the most common), intermediate, and dwarf forms. Plant tall forms in the middle or back of perennial borders or in mass plantings. Intermediate types look charming toward the front of the border. Dwarf forms bloom slightly earlier than tall bearded varieties and make nice additions to rock and specialty gardens and near the front of the border.

### IRIS X GERMANICA

**ZONES:** 3–10

**BLOOM TIME:** Early summer

**LIGHT:** Full sun

**HEIGHT:** 8–36 inches

**INTEREST:** Brilliant blooms; many sweetly fragrant

# SIBERIAN IRIS

## how to grow

Siberian iris needs full sun or light shade. Plant in any good garden soil, either moist or dry. In most soils you won't need to water much—the roots reach down deeply for moisture. However, the plants do require watering in sandy soils. Once established, Siberian irises never need dividing, but if you want to increase the number of plants (or reduce the size of large clumps), carefully dig them up in late summer, divide the crowns (this may require a large, sharp knife), and replant. Siberian iris grows vigorously in late summer and early fall; dividing in late summer allows divisions to reestablish themselves before winter. The only care required is deadheading and cutting down the foliage after two or three killing frosts in late fall.

Siberian iris ranks among the world's most loved garden plants for its abundant attractive flowers and handsome swordlike foliage that remains nice looking throughout the growing season. Through careful breeding, hybridizers have produced a host of flower colors in many shades of blue, purple, white, bicolors, and even yellow, such as this 'Butter and Sugar'. They have also doubled the size of the flowers of some varieties. The plants are impervious to pests and diseases, requiring almost no care. Barring unforeseen catastrophes, they'll grace your garden forever.

## IRIS SIBIRICA

**ZONES:** 3–8

**BLOOM TIME:** Early summer

**LIGHT:** Full sun to light shade

**HEIGHT:** 24–36 inches

**INTEREST:** Beautiful flowers of various colors; handsome green foliage

## where to grow

Grow Siberian irises in borders by themselves, in mixed borders, island beds, containers, and in the cutting garden. They are wonderful anywhere in your garden.

# ENGLISH LAVENDER

## how to grow

Lavender must be grown in full sun and well-drained soil that is slightly acidic to slightly alkaline. Winter wetness sitting around the crowns of plants is one of the main reasons it fails to thrive. It is also short-lived in the humid South. Shear the plants heavily in spring as soon as new growth starts to appear. Plants may be propagated from seeds, but named varieties must be reproduced from stem cuttings.

The fragrance of lavender has enjoyed a long history as a favored ingredient in soaps and perfumes. The lovely plants are a welcome addition to any garden for their beauty and fragrance. English lavender is a compact plant that usually grows to about 24 inches tall with very attractive silvery gray evergreen foliage. Flowers bloom on 12-inch stems that are ideal for cutting. The uses of lavender flowers are legendary, including dried arrangements, perfume, potpourri, wreaths, sachets, herb pillows, teas, and flavoring in oils and vinegars.

## where to grow

Lavender may be featured in an herb garden, toward the front of a mixed border, or on the south side of a house as a unique foundation planting. It is superb when planted with old-fashioned roses and unrivaled when used as a low hedge. It is also an excellent container plant for a sunny patio or deck. Plant lots for your use; otherwise you may find yourself tempted to strip the fragrant blossoms from the plants in your flower garden.

## LAVANDULA ANGUSTIFOLIA

**ZONES:** 5–10

**BLOOM TIME:** Midsummer

**LIGHT:** Full sun

**HEIGHT:** 12–36 inches

**INTEREST:** Wonderfully fragrant flowers; attractive, compact plants with silvery gray foliage

# SHASTA DAISY

## how to grow

This low-maintenance perennial performs best in rich, well-drained soil with liberal applications of organic matter. Full sun and regular watering during drought conditions are essential. Shasta daisies put on their best show if they are fertilized with a low-nitrogen plant food in early spring. Deadhead to keep the plants looking neat. Shasta daisies produce strong stems and do not need staking. Maintain plant vigor by dividing the crowns every 2 to 3 years. You can also start them from seeds that come remarkably true to variety.

For people who love white daisies, Shastas reign supreme. Previously known as *Chrysanthemum* x *superbum*, these hybrids were first created by the American plantsman Luther Burbank, and have become a mainstay of the perennial border. Shastas are tidy, well-behaved plants that require only a little attention to put on a delightful show of flowers for most of summer. The basal foliage remains evergreen during winter, adding a touch of rich dark green to the otherwise brown border. Since they bloom all summer and they last a long time in water, Shastas make superb cut flowers.

## LEUCANTHEMUM X SUPERBUM

**ZONES:** 4–9

**BLOOM TIME:** Summer

**LIGHT:** Full sun

**HEIGHT:** 12–36 inches

**INTEREST:** Large white daisies; attractive dark green foliage

## where to grow

Some say Shasta daisies belong in every sunny, well-drained perennial or mixed border. Like most white-flowered plants, they can be used to separate colors that clash. Since there are tall (36 inches) and short (12 inches) varieties, they can be used in the middle of a border or at the front. Shastas make excellent container plants for a patio or deck.

# GAY-FEATHER

## how to grow

Although tolerant of a wide variety of soil types, liatris thrives best in good garden soil that stays evenly moist and is well supplied with nutrients. Shoots are somewhat slow to appear in spring, so mark locations well and take care not to damage the tuberous roots when you're scratching around nearby. In rich soil or partial shade, the spikes grow taller and may require staking; be careful to avoid piercing the roots when setting stakes. Remove the entire spike to the top of the foliage after all the flowers have gone by—they open from the top downward. Liatris are all grown from seeds and are relatively inexpensive to purchase as dormant roots at garden centers.

Native to North America, liatris (it's more commonly known by its Latin name) is a must for the border. It provides a colorful, vertical accent, makes a superb cut flower (florists use it liberally), and is useful in dried arrangements. Liatris blends in well with perennials of many other shades; in fact it's hard to find a color it resents being next to. It's also a "no-brainer," requiring virtually no maintenance and no trouble whatsoever to keep it flourishing! Liatris attracts butterflies and bees to its blossoms and goldfinches to its seedpods in fall.

## where to grow

Liatris is ideal for the mixed border, providing a strong architectural element. Space permitting, it looks best planted in masses. Place in the middle or the front of a mixed planting so that you can enjoy it to the maximum, but also to get a close look at butterflies that swarm to feast on its nectar.

### LIATRIS SPICATA

**ZONES:** 3–8

**BLOOM TIME:** Mid- to late summer

**LIGHT:** Full sun

**HEIGHT:** 36–48 inches

**INTEREST:** Tall, rosy purple (or white) vertical spikes, attractive to bees and butterflies

# BEE BALM

## how to grow

Bee balm will grow in almost any soil, but it thrives best in those that are evenly moist. Drying out causes stress, which increases mildew; water well during hot, dry spells. Don't cut the stems back until spring, as the dead spikes are interesting in winter, especially against a snowscape; the foliage and seed heads retain their pungency even in a desiccated state. Bee balm spreads by underground runners and can be invasive; if it threatens to engulf your garden, just chop off edges of the clumps and transplant them, give them away, or compost them. Allow them to dry out completely before composting. Otherwise they'll grow and run rampant in the compost heap!

Bee balm is an invaluable plant for the perennial border. Its flowers come in a variety of shades and sit atop spicily scented foliage. Older varieties suffer from powdery mildew, but if plants are grown at the back of the border where the leaves are less obvious, this is not a problem worth concern. The leaves of this member of the mint family make a fine tea. 'Cambridge Scarlet' is shown here.

## MONARDA DIDYMA

**ZONES:** 4–8

**BLOOM TIME:** Mid- to late summer

**LIGHT:** Full sun to part shade

**HEIGHT:** 30–42 inches

**INTEREST:** Unique blooms in a range of colors; spicily fragrant foliage; attractive to butterflies and hummingbirds

## where to grow

Plant bee balm at the back of the perennial border or toward the center of an island bed. It also looks great in a wild garden or in a meadow where the free-spreading plants can romp gleefully. Since hummingbirds love the flowers, plant bee balm near your kitchen window so you can enjoy these flashing rainbows of color up close.

# CATMINT

## how to grow

Catmint is not terribly fussy about soil; it tolerates dry conditions better than most perennials. The taller forms may need staking, though their informal habit is appreciated by some. If you are the tidy type, place brushwood staking (see page 115) by the plants before they fall over. Cutting back the plants after the main flush of flowers has passed will ensure a strong second flush later in summer.

Catmint is a delightful plant with tall, wispy spikes of lavender-blue flowers over grayish green foliage that releases a pungent aroma when brushed. *Nepeta* x *faassenii* (shown here) is the most commonly grown variety. Catmint is invaluable for blending with soft colors and providing a backdrop for strong ones. It is easy to grow in most conditions except the high heat and humidity of the Deep South.

## where to grow

This plant belongs in every perennial border, shrub border, and rose garden, where it will add color and interest long after its companions have stopped blooming. There are very few colors that it doesn't look good planted alongside, but it is especially appealing near plants with pale yellow flowers.

### NEPETA X FAASSENII

**ZONES:** 3–8

**BLOOM TIME:** Summer

**LIGHT:** Full sun to light shade

**HEIGHT:** 18–24 Inches

**INTEREST:** Tall, long-lasting spikes of lavender-blue; pungent gray foliage

# PEONY

## how to grow

Peonies require rich soil with good drainage and lots of organic matter to hold moisture. Feed peonies in early spring and late fall with a low-nitrogen fertilizer. Double-flowered peonies tend to flop over and need to be staked. Place four to six sturdy 4-foot bamboo canes around each young plant. As the plant grows, lace soft string or green garden tape around the stakes. Make sure one string goes diagonally across the center of the plant to give the individual stems more support.

When professional plantsmen talk about essential plants for the garden, peonies rank near the top of the list. In part, their reputation comes from their dominant presence, in or out of flower. The foliage is a rich dark green that sets off the blossoms perfectly and, after the flowers have gone, gives the plants the demeanor of small shrubs. Peony blossoms come in variations of two forms: double and single. Double-flowered varieties bear large, dramatic flowers packed with showy petals, such as the 'Monsieur Jules Elie' shown here. Single-flowered varieties are less bold, with silky petals and graceful elegance. Most single-flowered peonies have strong, upright stems and, unlike double-flowered forms, rarely require staking. With proper care, peonies live longer than most other plants.

## PAEONIA

**ZONES:** 3–8

**BLOOM TIME:** Late spring

**LIGHT:** Full sun

**HEIGHT:** 36 inches

**INTEREST:** Very large, sometimes fragrant blossoms with single or double flowers; dark green, shrublike foliage with good fall color

## where to grow

Because peonies figure so prominently in a border, they should be set in place first, as accent points, with the rest of the design developed to complement them. As foundation plantings or low hedges, they're magnificent on their own and they make truly superb cut flowers. In warm areas where winters are mild, it is best to grow early-flowering varieties that finish growing before the heat of the summer.

# ORIENTAL POPPY

## how to grow

Oriental poppies prefer deeply dug, rich garden soil that their fleshy roots can penetrate easily. They tolerate dry soils, but not poor drainage. Give careful thought to where you want them—if they're moved later, new plants will appear from pieces of root left behind. Poppies prefer full sun. Add organic matter and a low-nitrogen fertilizer next to the crowns in late winter. Cut back the foliage or divide after plants go dormant.

For a few weeks each summer, Oriental poppies provide one of the most spectacular shows in the perennial garden. They produce a barrage of 4- to 6-inch blossoms in clear shades of pink, salmon, orange, red, or white, often with black markings at the centers. For sheer drama, a bed of poppies is a sight that's hard to beat. Poppy foliage appears very early in the year with large, rich green leaves that are rough to the touch. If planted in well-prepared soil, poppies become very long-lived plants that perform indefinitely without much care.

## where to grow

Oriental poppies look most dramatic when inter planted among colorful annuals and late-blooming perennials. These plants hide the yellow foliage as the poppies go dormant later in summer. Alongside poppies, plant a few irises or some pastel peonies to add softness beside the brilliant poppy flowers.

### PAPAVER ORIENTALE

**ZONES:** 2–7

**BLOOM TIME:** Early summer

**LIGHT:** Full sun

**HEIGHT:** 24–36 inches

**INTEREST:** Large, showy flowers in delicate to brilliant shades; interesting seedpods after petals have fallen

# BEARDTONGUE

## how to grow

Beardtongue requires ordinary but well-drained garden soil. It needs full sun in northern gardens, but prefers partial shade in the Southeast. Be certain to keep mulches away from the crown, as the plant will rot quickly if smothered. Remove dead flower spikes to encourage repeat blooming.

Though native to the Southwest and Mexico, beardtongue is perfectly hardy in the North and thrives in the heat and humidity of the Deep South. The small flowers, arranged along the stems (similar to foxglove), appear in shades of lavender, pink, red, purple, and white. Even in the darker colors, the effect is airy, and the plant adds a delicate presence to the late-June border among more flamboyant neighbors.

## PENSTEMON BARBATUS

**ZONES:** 3–9

**BLOOM TIME:** Early summer

**LIGHT:** Full sun

**HEIGHT:** 18–36 inches

**INTEREST:** Masses of tube-shaped flowers; recurrent bloom until frost

## where to grow

Place beardtongue anywhere toward the front of a mixed border where you want a touch of subtlety. Shorter-growing varieties are ideal for the rock garden. All sizes are stunning in cut flower arrangements.

# RUSSIAN SAGE

## how to grow

Grow Russian sage in any well-drained garden soil; the richer the soil, the more vigorously the plant will grow. Like many large plants, this one looks its best and performs best when it has room to spread out. It is impervious to pests and requires no maintenance except an annual pruning to 6 to 8 inches in late winter. In crowded situations it may require staking; this can be avoided by pinching out the growing tips of the main shoots in mid-June (three weeks earlier in the South).

Ignore the common name: Russian sage is not Russian at all, nor is it a sage (although it has a sagelike odor and belongs to the same family). It is, however, a superb plant with silvery gray foliage, clouds of lavender blossoms, and an enticing fragrance, all of which should win it a place in every sunny garden. It makes an excellent cut flower if cut when the flowers are young; however, the pungency may be somewhat overpowering in small, poorly ventilated rooms.

## where to grow

This plant's graceful presence makes it welcome anywhere in the garden. Give Russian sage a place of honor in the mixed border or the rose garden, or use it to enliven ho-hum foundation plantings. To enjoy Russian sage's fragrance and airy beauty all the more, be sure to plant some in a container on a patio, terrace, or deck.

### PEROVSKIA ATRIPLICIFOLIA

**ZONES:** 5–9

**BLOOM TIME:** Mid- to late summer

**LIGHT:** Full sun

**HEIGHT:** 36–60 inches

**INTEREST:** An elegant, pungently fragrant, shrubby perennial with lavender blossoms and gray foliage

# GARDEN PHLOX

## how to grow

Garden phlox requires well-drained soil that doesn't dry out, so be liberal with organic matter. Water thoroughly during dry spells using soaker hoses; avoid overhead sprinklers, which encourage the spread of mildew. Feed the plants in early spring and late fall with a low-nitrogen fertilizer; avoid overcrowding by removing half the new shoots as they appear. If mildew is a problem in your area, select varieties that are mildew resistant. In windy locations, stake plants with brushwood (see page 115) when they're about a foot high. Deadhead to prolong the blooming period.

Garden phlox has been a part of refined perennial gardens for decades. Today's varieties blend nostalgia and sophistication with a vigorous, no-nonsense nature that makes them beautiful and easy to grow. Garden phlox brightens up the late-summer border at a time when most perennials are past their peak. It comes in many colors, including bright lavender, pink, purple, red, and white. Some varieties have a central eye of a contrasting color. Most have a delightful sweet perfume. All are excellent cut flowers and may be cut as soon as at least a third of the blossoms have opened.

## PHLOX PANICULATA

**ZONES:** 4–8

**BLOOM TIME:** Late summer

**LIGHT:** Full sun

**HEIGHT:** 30–48 inches

**INTEREST:** Beautiful clusters of perky, fragrant flowers in many shades

## where to grow

Garden phlox is a classic plant for the middle of the border. Surround it with contrasting colors, but take care not to crowd it; garden phlox needs plenty of ventilation. In front, plant peonies; the rich foliage will showcase phlox's flowers but hide any foliage afflicted with powdery mildew. Be sure to plant enough phlox for cutting. It is a sweet-smelling addition to late-summer garden bouquets.

# MOSS PHLOX

## how to grow

Moss phlox requires full sun and any well-drained soil with low fertility (in other words, don't feed it). After flowering, cut the plants back with hedge shears to half their size to encourage compact growth. Propagate by dividing clumps as soon as the flowers fade.

Moss phlox's cheerful disposition makes it indispensable in the spring garden. After the drab gray of winter, when any color would be welcome, this creeping evergreen carpets the ground with bright flowers of blue, pink, purple, red, or white. Often found in old cemeteries, moss phlox spreads widely but not rampantly, doesn't mind being mowed during summer, and requires next to no care. All moss phlox selections have the same spreading habit. This is 'Purple Beauty'.

## where to grow

Use moss phlox as an edging for borders or along paths, or plant it in rock gardens or where it can cascade down a stone wall. It naturalizes well in lawns that are mowed long (no lower than 3 to 4 inches), and it also looks great in a spring window box. Moss phlox is lovely combined with dwarf spring bulbs in large pots or window boxes. After the moss phlox blooms in the window box, transplant it into the garden.

**PHLOX SUBULATA**

**ZONES:** 2–9

**BLOOM TIME:** Early spring

**LIGHT:** Full sun

**HEIGHT:** 6–9 inches

**INTEREST:** Carpets of flowers in many bright colors

# OBEDIENT PLANT

## how to grow

Obedient plant will grow in almost any garden soil, but in dry ones it will be shorter and less vigorous. Some varieties spread quickly, making them especially useful in meadow gardens of native or naturalized plants but disobedient nuisances in well-kept borders, especially in the South. Taller varieties require staking or cutting back to half their height in early July. Propagation is easy—dig up, divide, and replant the basal shoots in early spring. Obedient plant is not bothered by pests.

Obedient plant makes a bright splash of showy spikes of pink, purplish pink, or white blossoms in the late-summer garden. Flowers appear in spiky clusters atop square-stemmed shoots that are clothed with bright green foliage. The variegated form is simply dazzling. The plant gets its name from the fact that if you move individual flowers with your fingers to one side of the stem, they remain in their new location.

## PHYSOSTEGIA VIRGINIANA

**ZONES:** 2–9

**BLOOM TIME:** Late summer

**LIGHT:** Full sun

**HEIGHT:** 24–36 inches

**INTEREST:** Showy flower spikes in shades of pink and white

## where to grow

Obedient plant is perfect for a mixed border, where its color provides a welcome boost when earlier bloomers have lost their charm. Plant some in a cutting garden, too—the spikes hold up well in water and their obedience will impress your friends!

# BALLOON FLOWER

## how to grow

Balloon flower grows well in full sun except in the South, where it likes shelter from the afternoon rays. Plant in well-drained, average garden soil. Balloon flower gets a later spring start than many plants, so mark its location well to avoid damaging dormant crowns during early-spring garden work. Taller varieties may need staking; for a more natural look, grow them with baby's breath, whose foamy stems will intertwine with and hold up those of the balloon flower. To make bushier plants, pinch the growing tips when they reach 12 inches and don't worry about the "bleeding"; it will soon stop.

This tough relative of bellflower is a colorful, well-behaved plant that adds a bright note wherever it is planted. Before the flower buds open, they look like small balloons—hence the common name, balloon flower. The buds open into wide, upward-facing five-pointed chalices. Balloon flower is free flowering and long-lived, requires little or no maintenance, is useful as a cut flower, and suffers from no pests—what more could you ask of a flowering plant?

## where to grow

Plant balloon flower with impunity in mixed borders, rock gardens, and containers. It blends well with every other color. Shorter varieties are ideal for window boxes or for edging a path. They also make an astonishing ground cover, which from a distance looks like blue pools of water. Plant balloon flower with anything except the most vigorously spreading perennials.

## PLATYCODON GRANDIFLORUS

**ZONES:** 3–8

**BLOOM TIME:** Summer

**LIGHT:** Full sun in the North; part sun in the South

**HEIGHT:** 15–30 inches

**INTEREST:** Balloon-like flower buds followed by large, showy flowers over a long season

# BLACK-EYED SUSAN

## how to grow

Grow black-eyed Susan in any sunny spot in well-drained soil. In the Southeast it is best grown in part shade. Propagate by dividing the crowns in early spring as new shoots appear. Seed propagation is also possible, but the seedlings may differ from their parent. Black-eyed Susan is relatively pest-free and easy-care.

This selection of the black-eyed Susan is considered by some to be one of the world's great garden plants. In late summer, few plants produce as many blossoms. The flowers are 2 to 3 inches across and are a deep golden yellow with an almost black cone-shaped center. The plant's dazzling color and free-flowering habit make it a favorite with landscapers and gardeners who want to make a colorful impression. Black-eyed Susan is a low-maintenance perennial with a rugged persona inherited from its prairie roots.

### RUDBECKIA FULGIDA 'GOLDSTURM'

**ZONES:** 3–9

**BLOOM TIME:** Midsummer until hard frost

**LIGHT:** Full sun to light shade

**HEIGHT:** 18–30 inches

**INTEREST:** So many black-eyed golden daisies that they all but obscure the foliage

## where to grow

This is a must-grow plant that blends well with a surprisingly wide array of other colors. Use black-eyed Susan in the border, as a ground cover for sunny spots, or plant it in large groups in the flower or vegetable garden for cutting. As a container plant, it is unsurpassed for late-summer color. Enjoy the seed heads in winter as they poke through snow and provide food for seed-eating birds, then cut back the plants in early spring.

# PURPLE SAGE

## how to grow

All sages prefer average, well-drained garden soil and most tolerate drought rather well. The named varieties are best propagated by stem cuttings in early summer, before they flower. They are easy to grow from collected or purchased seeds, but the offspring won't be identical to the parent.

Purple sage is a free-flowering plant with dark-colored blossoms that contrast pleasantly with most other shades. *Salvia* x *sylvestris* is often sold as (and is very similar to) *Salvia* x *superba.* Both are choice hybrids that make outstanding garden plants. Both have narrow, dark blue to purple flower spikes on stems that grow from 18 to 36 inches tall, depending on the variety. The foliage is a pleasing gray-green and clothes the well-branched stems. There is a great deal of confusion in catalogs about the correct names for these plants—they hybridize so readily that growers are sometimes not sure what they have.

## where to grow

Sage is drought tolerant and performs well both in cool northern climates and in hot ones. In the Deep South, it prefers part shade; tall varieties have a tendency to lose their tidy habit in part shade, though.

### SALVIA X SYLVESTRIS

**ZONES:** 4–10

**BLOOM TIME:** Summer

**LIGHT:** Full sun

**HEIGHT:** 18–36 inches

**INTEREST:** Rich, dark bluish violet spikes on compact, well-behaved plants

# PINCUSHION FLOWER

## how to grow

Pincushion flower requires sun and well-drained soil that is slightly acidic to slightly alkaline. Provide extra water during dry spells. To encourage more abundant blooming, remove dead flower heads regularly—it's a small chore for a plant that gives so much in return. Propagation is by division, but who would want to give up so many blossoms for a single season when purchased plants are relatively inexpensive?

Pincushion flower's prolific blooming habit has made it one of the most popular perennials around. Its lovely lavender-blue, white, or lilac-pink 2-inch blossoms first appear in early summer and continue until hard frost—in mild climates it continues to bloom during winter. Of course, butterflies love it too!

## SCABIOSA CAUCASICA

**ZONES:** 3–8

**BLOOM TIME:** All summer to frost

**LIGHT:** Full sun

**HEIGHT:** 18–24 inches

**INTEREST:** Compact plant that blooms its head off with lavender-blue, white, or lilac-pink flowers

## where to grow

This unsurpassed bloomer is ideal for containers or for the front of a border. It also looks stunning planted in a bed with small ornamental grasses. Its ability to flower during the shorter days of winter makes it an ideal pot plant for a cool conservatory or greenhouse—with an occasional excursion indoors for special events. Because pincushion flower blooms so long, locate it with other plants that span the growing season from spring to fall, including daylilies, Carpathian bellflowers, mallow, purple sages, hollyhocks, and Stokes' asters.

# SEDUM

## how to grow

'Autumn Joy' grows in almost any soil and is completely maintenance-free, pest-free, and absolutely reliable—in other words, you can't miss with this garden favorite. The rusty brown seed heads are one of the joys of winter gardens. Plants often self-sow. Watch for the small plants to appear in the garden and transplant to a new location. Large clumps should be divided every 3 to 4 years so they don't become weak and floppy.

A showy sedum cultivar, 'Autumn Joy' is one of the most popular flowering perennials of late summer. It has such a strong personality that it dominates its surroundings. Green buds appear in late summer and look like broccoli heads (but don't eat them). Gradually they turn light pink, mature to a warm pink, then become rusty red and finally a rich brown. The flowers are long lasting and dry well for winter arrangements. The fleshy foliage is an attractive grayish green and very succulent. In winter, lightly dusted with snow, 'Autumn Joy' adds a strong architectural feature to the garden.

## where to grow

It is probably impossible (and maybe illegal) to have a garden without at least one clump of 'Autumn Joy'. Many gardeners can't resist planting lots of it—in perennial and mixed borders, by itself in huge drifts, or in containers. Plant enough to use for flower arrangements. It is a spectacular addition.

### SEDUM 'AUTUMN JOY'

**ZONES:** 3–9

**BLOOM TIME:** Late summer to fall

**LIGHT:** Full to part sun

**HEIGHT:** 18–24 inches

**INTEREST:** Abundant flowers that vary in shades of pink and red as the season passes; much loved by butterflies and bees; attractive, succulent foliage

# LAMB'S EARS

## how to grow

Lamb's ears requires well-drained garden soil, so avoid overhead watering, especially in hot, humid weather. Buried soaker hoses work best. In the Southeast, heat and humidity and frequent thunderstorms keep the foliage wet. As a result, the plants "melt out" in summer but bounce back in fall. During the winter they remain fresh and evergreen, which makes them worth a place in the garden despite their summer sulk.

The soft, furry, silver-gray leaves of lamb's ears are irresistible to children and sensualists. Its 12- to 15-inch flower spikes are not showy (the small lavender-pink blooms are almost hidden by the silver-gray stem leaves) and are thought to distract from the more appealing foliage. For this reason, many gardeners remove them as soon as they appear. Plants are spreading, but not invasively so, and gradually form clumps measuring 3 to 4 feet across.

### STACHYS BYZANTINE

**ZONES:** 5–9

**BLOOM TIME:** Early summer

**LIGHT:** Full to part sun

**HEIGHT:** 6–8 inches (foliage); 12–15 inches (flowers)

**INTEREST:** Large, velvety silver-gray leaves

## where to grow

Lamb's ears is usually planted at the edges of borders or in spots where it can spill over paths and terraces— the better to have its leaves petted by all who pass. While not a star in its own right, it acts as the perfect background for colorful companions; any moderate-sized plant makes a good neighbor. Lamb's ears can be used as a ground cover under roses or among dwarf conifers, where it is content to play a supporting role.

# SPEEDWELL

## how to grow

Speedwell prefers average, well-drained garden soil and will tolerate dry conditions. It thrives in southern heat, but also flourishes in the cool North. If grown in part shade, it may flop over, so support the plant with short lengths of brushwood. Otherwise the only care required is deadheading.

Speedwell, more commonly known by its botanical name, *Veronica*, is very popular for its showy flower spikes and its prodigious blooming habit. 'Royal Candles' is shown here. It is remarkably tough in both the cold winters of the North and the heat and humidity of the Southeast. Speedwell is an easy grower and is virtually trouble-free. The blooms last well in water if cut when half the flowers on a spike are open.

## where to grow

Plant speedwell at the edges of perennial borders, spilling over paths and stone walls, and in rock gardens, window boxes, and containers. Don't forget to plant some to cut for baskets of blossoms all summer long.

### VERONICA

**ZONES:** 3–10

**BLOOM TIME:** All summer until frost

**LIGHT:** Full to part sun

**HEIGHT:** 12–24 inches

**INTEREST:** Masses of blue, pink, or white flower spikes

# BEST TIPS
## FOR GROWING PERENNIALS

### removing slugs

Slugs are ever present in moist garden spots, but you can reduce their impact. Avoid poison slug baits and sprays that can wash away. Remove slugs instead.

- Pick them off plants at night when they feed. Use rubber gloves so they don't "slime" you.

- Trap them in grapefruit halves (empty) placed upside down throughout the garden. Check and dispose of any containing slugs.

- Sink margarine tubs into the soil with rims at ground level. Fill ¾ full with beer. Empty when "traps" contain several slugs.

# root cuttings

When stem cuttings are not possible, use root cuttings to get new plants exactly like the parent. Plants to propagate in this manner include phlox, sea holly, globe thistle, and Oriental poppies.

1. In midfall, fill a flowerpot with a rooting medium that is two parts pasteurized potting soil, one part coarse sand. Press evenly to firm the soil.

2. Carefully dig up the plant and choose no more than one-third of the thickest roots. With a very sharp knife, cut off the roots close to the crown of the plant. Take care to keep the ends closest to the crown together, as new shoots arise only from this "top" end.

3. Cut the roots into 2- to 3-inch lengths—arranging so the root tops all face the same direction.

4. Make a hole that is large enough to insert each root piece upright ("top" end up) in the rooting medium without bending or snapping it.

5. Water and place the container in a temperature of 45° to 55°F. No light is needed until new shoots begin to push up through the soil.

6. In spring, separate the new plants and plant them in the garden. Protect from direct sunlight for a week.

## staking tall plants

To stake tall plants, cut lengths of twiggy brushwood (such as birch) in early spring before leaves appear. Make them 1 foot shorter than the plants requiring staking. When a plant has reached half its normal height, place stakes in the ground all around it. Surround with garden twine if necessary.

## controlling pesky bugs

Japanese beetles are somewhat fond of Shasta daisies. One of the surest ways to get rid of these pests is to pick them off early in the morning while the beetles are groggy (they do have a very active social life). Wear rubber gloves if you find their touch distasteful. To drown the captured beetles, drop them into a jar filled with water and a shot of dishwashing detergent.

## shady sites

Within the world of shade gardening, you'll find plants that accept all degrees of shade while others are tolerant only of certain types. Your garden will flourish best when you match your perennials with the kinds of shade that are cast over the planting beds during different seasons.

- Relegate your most sun-sensitive plants to areas of deepest shade—beneath heavy tree canopies, on the sunless north side of buildings and fences, or under overhangs where no sun penetrates.

- Plants that must have brighter light but no direct sun do well in moderate shade provided by evergreen trees with lower branches removed, or by clumps of deciduous trees, such as those in woodlands. Widely spaced trees with few low branches create part shade. No sun reaches directly underneath at midday, but the open space all around allows morning or afternoon sun to flow beneath their canopies.

- Lighter shade is filtered or dappled, and is found beneath uncrowded, open-branched deciduous trees.

- If your perennials will flower more heavily in a bit of sun but cannot tolerate severe intensities, try to plant them in either part or lightly filtered shade. Remove lower tree limbs to let in more indirect light.

## winter protection

Mulching during the growing season provides many benefits for perennials (see page 4), but mulching for winter protection is a different kind of safeguard.

Many plants need winter protection to guard them against repeated thawing and freezing. Without insulation, shallow-rooted and freshly set plants are inevitably harmed when the movement of the soil heaves them out of the ground. Winter protection also prevents plants from drying out in cold winter winds.

1. After the ground is well frozen, cover the entire plant with straw, salt-marsh hay, or pine needles.

2. Add a layer of pine boughs or other available evergreen prunings; don't overlook the branches of a discarded Christmas tree.

3. In spring, at about the time the forsythia blooms, remove the protective materials. You can shake off the pine needles or evergreen leaves and spread out the straw or hay to use as the first layer of spring mulch. Keep it away from the crowns of your plants where the new shoots are emerging.

## deadheading

To increase flowering in many plants, remove flowers as soon as they have passed their peak. Cut down to the next leaf or branch on the spent flower stem. This prevents the formation of seeds and encourages the plant to produce more flowers. The plants look better, too.

BEST
TIPS

## propagation from stem cuttings

Rooting stem cuttings is an easy form of vegetative propagation when plants grow roots easily. It's often easier to get more clumps using this method than by dividing existing clumps. Try it with spotted dead nettle, periwinkle, and upright bugle, to name a few.

1. Remove the lower pair of leaves from 4- to 6-inch nonflowering shoots. Stick the cut ends of the shoots in a glass of water on a sunless windowsill. Allow the shoots to develop roots for 4 to 6 weeks.

2. Transplant the shoots to the desired outdoor location and water thoroughly. Cover with weighted down newspaper for a few days to shade them.

3. Remove the newspaper for a short time in the morning or late afternoon; increase the time by a little each day, until the new plants are perky enough to stand on their own.

## keeping snails and slugs out

You can protect small plantings, raised beds, and containers from slugs or snails by installing copper barriers. Rolls of very thin copper strips are available from garden centers and supply catalogs. Install these along the edge of containers or planters, or around small plantings. Slugs and snails can't crawl across copper. Wear gloves when handling the copper strips, because the edges are razor sharp.

## planning ahead

Ephemerals are plants that disappear completely after blooming. Many spring wildflowers such as leopard's bane and Virginia bluebells fit this description. Spring ephemerals leave a "hole" in the border when they go dormant in midsummer.

These holes are best filled with tender bulbs or annuals. However, you can't simply install these plants at the beginning of the growing season. To fill the holes, you must plan ahead, since in spring the ephemerals will occupy the space.

1. In spring, pot up impatiens, dahlias, caladiums, or similar plants in 6- to 8-inch flowerpots to give them time to get established.

2. When the spring ephemeral starts to look punky, trim yellowing foliage. (Leave the foliage in place until it has yellowed to ensure that plants will have enough energy to bloom the following spring.)

3. Hide the ephemeral with the potted filler plant placed in front.

## treating cut flowers that bleed

Balloon flowers (also blue stars, butterfly weeds, some bellflowers, and Oriental poppies) bleed when they are cut. To stop the bleeding, singe the end of each stem immediately after cutting with a quick touch from the flame of a match or a lighter. Flaming the stem ends of these plants will extend their vase life; it will not enhance flowers that don't bleed.

BEST
TIPS

# BEST PERENNIALS FOR SHADE

# LADYBELLS

## how to grow

Ladybells prefers deep, well-dug soil with good drainage and liberal amounts of organic matter worked in before planting. In early spring, mulch with 2 inches of leaf compost around the crowns to maintain a moderately rich, evenly moist soil. Ladybells forms new plants by self-sowing, but it is noninvasive, so it won't become a garden pest.

This valuable bellflower relative from China is one of the few plants that bloom well in summer shade. Pretty spikes of purplish blue bell-shaped blooms hang down like Chinese lanterns along the 30- to 36-inch vertical stems of ladybells. The bloom-laden spikes sit atop rich green foliage, flowering freely from mid- to late summer. This low-maintenance plant spreads but is not invasive and is long-lived in areas with the right growing conditions. More heat tolerant than most of its relatives, this cheerful perennial fares well in the Southeast and much of the Southwest (except desert areas).

### ADENOPHORA CONFUSA

**ZONES:** 3–9

**BLOOM TIME:** Mid- to late summer

**LIGHT:** Part shade

**HEIGHT:** 30–36 inches

**INTEREST:** Upright spikes of purple-blue flowers for weeks

## where to grow

Equally happy in part shade and full sun, ladybells is suitable for a naturalized planting beside a shady walk under trees that have had their lower branches removed. It is also a good choice for more formal planting in a mixed border with perennials and shrubs. Since it is an excellent addition to floral arrangements, plant extra for cutting. Choose your location carefully, because the deep-growing, fleshy roots of ladybells resent being transplanted once established, and they usually outlive the gardener.

# UPRIGHT BUGLE

## how to grow

Although it prefers partial shade, upright bugle will tolerate sun if planted in rich, moist soil. It grows best in moist soil (never waterlogged) that is rich in organic matter. Before planting, incorporate lots of leaf compost or peat moss, especially if the soil is light and sandy. Mulching with 2 to 3 inches of leaf compost will keep soil moist and maintain a high humus level, a condition this plant favors. Keep plants looking neat by removing spent blossoms at the end of the bloom season. Plants can be divided easily almost any time, providing the soil is kept moist and the transplants are shaded from hot sun.

Upright bugle has showy 6- to 9-inch spikes of rich violet-blue blossoms and puts on quite a show when in bloom. After flowering, it makes a refined ground cover of dark green foliage. Unlike the more familiar common bugle, which is widely used as a ground cover because it spreads like a weed, this cousin is a well-mannered, clump-forming plant. It is easy to grow and requires little maintenance once established.

## where to grow

The most attractive plantings of upright bugle are those where large groups are situated in light shade under trees and large bushes. Upright bugle is ideal for a woodland garden, as well as on the east side of buildings, where it is shaded by the building during the brightest part of the day. Use it with other ground covers for a contrast in texture with a bonus of spring flowers.

AJUGA
PYRAMIDALIS
**ZONES:** 3–10
**BLOOM TIME:** Late spring
**LIGHT:** Part shade
**HEIGHT:** 6–9 inches
**INTEREST:** Attractive ground cover with spikes of violet-blue flowers and a tidy, noninvasive habit

# LADY'S MANTLE

## how to grow

Lady's mantle prefers part shade, but it can also be grown in full sun—provided that the soil doesn't dry out in the heat of summer. It is happiest in soil that is rich in organic matter and holds moisture well but is also well drained. Lady's mantle requires little maintenance; the only chore is to remove the spent blossoms after they finally cease to delight the eye. In the Southeast, this plant sometimes succumbs to high humidity, so it is best to place it in areas where it has the necessary part shade and excellent air movement to keep it happy.

In early summer, lady's mantle covers itself with long-lasting chartreuse flowers, a unique shade in the plant world and one that complements almost every other garden hue. The starry blossoms make great cut flowers that remain attractive for 2 to 3 weeks. Its beautifully shaped large leaves are a pleasing light green and have the delightful habit of trapping jewel-like beads of water after rain or irrigation. The Latin name *Alchemilla* is derived from an association with ancient alchemists, who believed this plant had many medicinal properties.

## ALCHEMILLA MOLLIS

**ZONES:** 3–9

**BLOOM TIME:** Summer

**LIGHT:** Part shade

**HEIGHT:** 18–24 inches

**INTEREST:** Handsome light green foliage and abundant, long-lasting clusters of greenish yellow flowers that blend with just about every color

## where to grow

Lady's mantle can be grown in woodland gardens, along a shady path, or as a foundation plant in front of evergreen bushes. Or try it in a mixed border, as a ground cover, or in a bed by itself. Lady's mantle is a great neighbor for plants of almost any hue. Use it to complement flowers in cool colors such as blue, lavender, or white, or as a cool companion for hot yellow, orange, red, or purple hues. Cut flowers will never be missed from large plantings of lady's mantle because it blooms profusely.

# JAPANESE ANEMONE

## how to grow

Set out hybrid anemones in spring or fall in a well-drained, slightly acidic, loamy soil in light shade or full sun. Before planting, incorporate a slow-release fertilizer into the soil along with generous portions of leaf mold, compost, or peat moss; adding a 1- to 2-inch layer of mulch helps preserve moisture. These perennials have little drought tolerance and will show browned foliage if moisture is lacking. During hot, dry summers, you may need to give them some extra water.

Japanese anemone is the catchall name for a large group of late-summer- and fall-blooming hybrids. These heavy-blooming shade plants produce either single or double, pink or white blossoms that float like butterflies on wiry stems above clumps of maple-like foliage. For the late-season garden, Japanese anemones offer some of the brightest color spots. The yellow-centered, saucer-shaped blossoms are up to 3 inches across on many varieties and stand 3 to 5 feet tall; foliage clumps are about 2 feet high and wide.

## where to grow

Lightly shaded sites are best for Japanese anemones. With some protection from sun, the plants grow robustly; they can even tolerate some neglect in regions where rainfall is plentiful. The more vigorous varieties spread by underground rhizomes to form colonies, a welcome addition to naturalized gardens. Plant small drifts of anemones in borders where the late-season foliage will cover holes left by spring bulbs or perennials that have died back. Fit them, also, into bays in shrub borders with azaleas or viburnums; in these locations, you may need to curb their spread.

### ANEMONE X HYBRID

**ZONES:** 4–9

**BLOOM TIME:** Late summer and early fall

**LIGHT:** Part shade

**HEIGHT:** 24–48 inches

**INTEREST:** Colorful blooms that are welcome in shade gardens when little else is blooming

# SNOWDROP ANEMONE

## how to grow

Snowdrop anemone grows most vigorously in rich, light, and moist but well-drained soil. After bloom in summer, this species can tolerate some dryness; it also withstands more alkaline soils than do other anemones. If you cut the flower stems to the ground just after the blossoms fade, snowdrop anemones are likely to reward you with a second bloom in fall. Stems left standing develop white, wooly seed heads.

Of the many and varied anemones, one of the most delightful is that spring charmer, the snowdrop anemone. Its small, cup-shaped flowers in pure white are dotted with tufts of yellow stamens in the centers. Each of the 2-inch blossoms stands alone atop wiry, 18-inch flower stalks that rise out of 12-inch mounds of divided blue-green leaves. This fast-growing perennial owes its strength to tough underground rhizomes that want to creep beyond the original planting and colonize shaded sites.

## ANEMONE SYLVESTRIS

**ZONES:** 4–9

**BLOOM TIME:** Spring to early summer

**LIGHT:** Part shade

**HEIGHT:** 12–18 inches

**INTEREST:** Solitary, nodding snow-white flowers that are slightly fragrant and bloom nonstop

## where to grow

This small sylvan native is perfect for naturalizing along the edges of deciduous woodlands. Its fast-growing nature makes its usefulness limited in a perennial garden, however, since it readily becomes too aggressive if conditions are ideal. You will appreciate snowdrop anemones most if you plant them where their runners can be contained or where they won't overpower more well-behaved perennials. In place of a lawn and where no traffic is allowed, this species makes a good ground cover among shrubs and low trees.

# JACK-IN-THE-PULPIT

## how to grow

Jack-in-the-pulpit is anything but fussy and requires no maintenance. To keep it happy, plant in humus-rich soil that retains moisture without staying soggy. Jack-in-the-pulpit can be planted or transplanted at any time of the year when the soil is workable—just add lots of organic matter (leaf compost or peat moss) before planting. To form new colonies, transplant the seedlings that spring up around the parent plants.

Jack-in-the-pulpit is widespread in the woods of the eastern United States. Heights and colors vary, even in the same area. "Jack" (the reproductive organs, also called the spadix, of this fanciful plant) stands in a "pulpit" (a cuplike structure that is covered by a spathe, a colorful bract that arches over). The unusual blossoms remain attractive for several weeks before the fruits (mature Jacks) swell to a bright emerald green, then turn to scarlet red. Although not poisonous, the fruits cause a severe irritation to the mouth. Since the fruits look like candy, take care to keep small children away. Native Americans used the tubers to make a starchy food by boiling out the irritant and grinding and drying the mash into a type of flour.

## where to grow

Jack-in-the-pulpit is a wildflower that belongs in woodland or shady gardens, where it will put on an unusual show. Since it will tolerate heavy shade, try it on the north side of buildings and under evergreen trees. It looks really striking planted amid low-growing ferns that will hide the bare spot left when the Jack goes dormant in midsummer. This plant seeds itself to form a colony, but it will never become an invasive pest.

### ARISAEMA TRIPHYLLUM

**ZONES:** 4–9

**BLOOM TIME:** Late spring to early summer

**LIGHT:** Part to full shade

**HEIGHT:** 12–30 inches

**INTEREST:** Exotic flowers in shades of green and purple; brilliant scarlet fruit clusters follow

# GOAT'S BEARD

## how to grow

For goat's beard to thrive, it requires humus-rich soil that doesn't dry out in summer. Be sure to enhance the soil with lots of organic matter at planting time and make sure that the soil is well moistened before adding mulch to hold in moisture. Water well during summer dry spells. Staking isn't necessary except in areas that get hit with frequent torrential downpours when the plant is in bloom. Maintenance is easy—remove spent blossoms and cut down the plant when it dies back in late fall.

Goat's beard has been warmly welcomed into many shady gardens because of its huge, feathery plumes of creamy white flowers. Like its relative astilbe (see pages 138 to 141), it is equally happy in full sun, but only where summers are not too hot and the soil is consistently moist throughout the growing season. In its native habitat, goat's beard even grows in wet, marshy areas, so it is almost impossible to overwater it in your garden. Like its stubborn namesake, the mature plant requires a backhoe or dynamite to force it out of the ground; it is best left where first established.

## ARUNCUS DIOICUS

**ZONES:** 4–9

**BLOOM TIME:** Early summer

**LIGHT:** Part shade

**HEIGHT:** 4–6 feet

**INTEREST:** Attractive, fernlike pale green foliage and spectacular plumes of creamy white flowers

## where to grow

Goat's beard is a large plant that requires lots of room. This elegant plant will grace any property that has high shade in the afternoon—under tall trees, at the north side of a tall shrub, or in a woodland garden. Its stately presence is wonderful in the back of a border where, as it matures, it will dominate its neighbors for several weeks. It sets off other tall plants such as delphiniums (don't keep the soil wet around these plants, though!) and provides a foil for herbaceous peonies, the real showoffs of the plant world. For a more subtle and refined combination, plant Siberian iris in front of goat's beard.

# EUROPEAN WILD GINGER

## how to grow

Shade is a must—either light or fairly heavy. (See page 116 for an explanation of different types of shade.) As with many shade lovers, rich, moist, but well-drained soil that doesn't dry out in summer is also essential. Work lots of leaf compost or peat moss into the soil before planting, then mulch with a thin layer of leaf compost in late fall or late winter. Water well during dry spells in summer. Unlike with some ground covers, there is no need to remove the spent flowers of European wild ginger to maintain its attractiveness. In addition, the leaf cover is enough to suppress most weeds. Seedlings often appear under large clumps; transplant them as soon as they are large enough to handle.

European wild ginger is an easy-care, spreading foliage plant that looks good all season long. It spreads in a noninvasive manner, making it an ideal ground cover for areas with part or full shade. The flowers are a nondescript greenish brown. Tucked under the foliage, they play no role in the ornamental value of this evergreen plant. The roots smell of ginger when bruised or cut—hence the common name. Clusters of the shiny, round leaves make a perfect backdrop for a nosegay of violets or a bouquet of other tiny flowers.

## where to grow

Wild ginger is a valuable ground cover to plant alongside woodland paths and at the front of woodland gardens. The elegant foliage is equally at home in more formal and shady urban settings. To create an exciting interplay of textures, place it alongside low-growing ferns, dwarf astilbes, and dwarf hostas. It is especially pleasing when underplanted with small spring-flowering bulbs such as crocus or Siberian squill.

### ASARUM EUROPAEUM

**ZONES:** 4–8

**BLOOM TIME:** Inconspicuous flowers

**LIGHT:** Part to full shade

**HEIGHT:** 6 inches

**INTEREST:** Heart-shaped, shiny dark green leaves that make a very desirable mat-forming evergreen ground cover

# HYBRID ASTILBE

## how to grow

Astilbe requires humus-rich soil that retains moisture yet is fast draining. Some varieties are more drought tolerant than others, but all must have adequate moisture in either sun or shade or their foliage will shrivel and brown. Avoid planting astilbe in boggy conditions; it will succumb to rot in too much water, especially while dormant in winter. Incorporate ample amounts of well-decomposed compost, aged manure, or leaf mold into the soil before planting. After planting, add a 2- to 3-inch layer of mulch—pine needles or shredded bark—over the surface to hold in moisture. The browned flower spikes remain attractive in autumn, but your astilbes will look tidier and bloom more heavily the next year if you trim off the dried flower stalks.

Astilbe puts on the most spectacular show of any shade-loving plant. When in bloom, 12- to 24-inch-long, many-branched flower spikes shine brilliantly in lavender to rose-pink, in blood red to salmon and magenta, and in creamy, rosy, and snowy white. The lacy, fernlike foliage grows in clumps 2 to 4 feet high and nearly as wide. It remains attractive from its first appearance in spring until it is covered by winter frost or snow. Some selections have stunning bronze leaves.

## ASTILBE X ARENDSII

**ZONES:** 4–9

**BLOOM TIME:** Summer

**LIGHT:** Part shade

**HEIGHT:** 22–48 inches

**INTEREST:** Plumes of flowers in many shades of pink, red, or white; one of the most rugged garden plants

## where to grow

Hybrid astilbe belongs in every border with moist soil. Its glossy foliage adds refinement to any planting all season long. Enjoy months of color by selecting those with early, midseason, and late bloom periods. When introducing astilbes into a woodland habitat, choose varieties with a loose, arching habit; reserve the stiffly upright growers for more formal locations in borders or along foundations.

# DWARF ASTILBE

## how to grow

Check the soil moisture throughout summer wherever you plant your astilbes. Their shallow roots are easily damaged by dry conditions, and you may need to irrigate if summer rains are scarce. All species like their roots shaded with mulch and their top growth in shade for several hours during midday unless you live in a cool, coastal area where the soil stays constantly moist.

This group of dwarf astilbes is sometimes called the star astilbes for the starlike blossoms that grace their dense, pyramidal flower plumes. The leafy clumps attain a height of little more than 1 foot, have small individual leaves, and are somewhat slower growing than other species; the foliage of some varieties is tinted bronze or burgundy. If you're tempted to cut the plumy flowers for indoor arrangements, you'll be happy with them only briefly, for their blossoms quickly fade. After bloom in the garden, the browned seed heads continue to decorate plants. You can leave them standing throughout winter, or you can cut them back after the first hard frost. Astilbes are most effective when massed in groups of five or more to create swaths of color running through your garden beds.

## where to grow

These low-growing astilbes are wonderfully versatile in the garden. Plant them in combination with other perennials and ferns in low borders or use them as accents alongside a garden bench, under small trees, or in a rock garden. You can create spectacular effects by alternating with taller plants. If you introduce astilbes into a woodland scene, choose varieties with a loose, arching habit; reserve the stiffly upright growers for more formal locations in borders or along foundations.

### ASTILBE SIMPLICIFOLIA

**ZONES:** 4–9

**BLOOM TIME:** Summer

**LIGHT:** Part shade

**HEIGHT:** 12–18 inches

**INTEREST:** Plumes of flowers in many shades of pink, red, or white; one of the most rugged garden plants

# JAPANESE PAINTED FERN

## how to grow

Grow in rich, well-drained soil with medium moisture. Trim leaves to the ground in late fall or early spring. Since it can form dense colonies, it can be divided in early spring, every 3 to 4 years.

This easy-to-grow fern was the North American Perennial Plant Association's Perennial Plant of the Year in 2004.

## ATHYRIUM NIPONICUM VAR. PICTUM

**ZONES:** 4–8

**BLOOM TIME:** Does not flower; foliage is most interesting in spring

**LIGHT:** Partial to full shade

**HEIGHT:** 12–18 inches

**INTEREST:** Arching, silvery-gray fronds

## where to grow

Grow this fern in sheltered, shady spots near water such as streams and ponds. With a little bit of direct sun in the morning or late in the day, the colors become more saturated.

# HARDY BEGONIA

## how to grow

Hardy begonia does best in rich, moist, well-drained soil in part shade, but it tolerates even heavy shade. You can extend its blooming time by deadheading (see p. 117). Mulching will help to protect the plant for the winter, especially in the northernmost zones of its hardiness.

Hardy begonia has dainty pink flowers (or white ones in the cultivar 'Alba', shown here). The plant appears later in spring than others, so be careful to not inadvertently pull it out when doing spring cleaning!

## where to grow

Hardy begonia tolerates heavy shade, so plant in a shade or woodland garden, along with ferns and hostas. It also works well in containers. It can also handle moist locations, such as near streams. If you don't like where it's growing, go ahead and move it; since it has shallow roots, it is easy to transplant successfully.

**BEGONIA GRANDIS**

**ZONES:** 6–9

**BLOOM TIME:** Midsummer to fall

**LIGHT:** Partial to full shade

**HEIGHT:** 1½ to 2 feet

**INTEREST:** Dangling pink flower sprays and heart-shaped foliage

# HEARTLEAF BERGENIA

## how to grow

Heartleaf bergenia adapts to a wide range of conditions. It grows best in moist, slightly acidic soil that is rich in organic matter. In cool regions in moist soil, it can grow in full sun, but the foliage looks best under the filtered light of high trees. In the South, grow heartleaf bergenia in part to full shade. In cold regions with unreliable snow cover, protect plants in winter with a thick layer of straw or salt hay added in late fall.

Heartleaf bergenia is one of the best-kept secrets of shade gardening. Native to regions of central Asia, this hardy plant has thick, shiny leaves that remain green through winter, even in cold northern areas. In spring, nodding clusters of pink, white, or rosy red flowers rise on succulent stalks to peek above the mantle of leaves.

### BERGENIA CORDIFOLIA

**ZONES:** 3–9

**BLOOM TIME:** Spring

**LIGHT:** Part shade

**HEIGHT:** 18 inches

**INTEREST:** Attractive clusters of pink, white, or red flowers above handsome, glossy evergreen foliage

## where to grow

Heartleaf bergenia can be used in the same manner as hosta (pages 178 to 179). Plant as an edging along walkways or to define the front of the perennial border. It makes an excellent ground cover under deciduous trees and is a good accent plant for shady rock or water gardens. Heartleaf bergenia is especially nice in clumps along a woodland trail in the company of primroses and ferns.

# SIBERIAN BUGLOSS

## how to grow

Siberian bugloss requires well-drained soil that is rich in organic matter to help it retain moisture. Plants will tolerate morning sun in moist sites and need more shade in drier sites. Mulch well and water plants thoroughly during summer dry spells. Slugs can be a problem, but apart from dealing with this pest, Siberian bugloss requires no other maintenance.

This rugged perennial has tiny, brilliant sky blue flowers like forget-me-nots (unrelated) that twinkle against its large, dark green, heart-shaped foliage. When in bloom, Siberian bugloss is stunning; for the remainder of the season, its foliage adds texture and an interesting leaf shape to any shade garden. This tough, low-maintenance plant makes a fine ground cover.

## where to grow

Rugged Siberian bugloss is at home at the edge of a woodland garden as well as along a shady path. It looks superb planted with late-flowering narcissus (especially jonquil), because they flower at similar times. Underplant it with true lilies to provide summer color. This lovely perennial makes an interesting ground cover under small-growing shrubs such as deciduous azalea, red twig dogwood, and sweet pepperbush.

### BRUNNERA MACROPHYLLA

**ZONES:** 3–10

**BLOOM TIME:** Spring

**LIGHT:** Part shade

**HEIGHT:** 12–18 inches

**INTEREST:** Tiny blue flowers over heart-shaped leaves

# TURTLEHEAD

## how to grow

Turtlehead prefers moist, rich soil. Though it can tolerate nearly full shade, it may need to be staked if grown in deep shade. Prune back the stems in early spring so that they don't get too tall. It has no significant pest or disease issues.

The flowers of *Chelone*, which sit atop spikes that rise above the dark foliage, look similar to snapdragons and are named for their resemblance to turtles with their mouths open.

### CHELONE LYONII

**ZONES:** 3–8

**BLOOM TIME:** Late summer to fall

**LIGHT:** Full sun to partial shade

**HEIGHT:** 2–4 feet

**INTEREST:** Two-lipped pink-purple flowers at top of spikes

## where to grow

Turtlehead does well in shade and woodland gardens, particularly near water, as it tolerates poorly drained soil. It pairs nicely with small shrubs.

# FAIRY CANDLES

## how to grow

Fairy candles must have rich, moist soil that drains well. In dry locations the leaves turn brown and may drop off, so mulch well and water heavily during dry spells. Staking isn't usually necessary, but overfeeding with plant food may cause the stems to grow so luxuriantly that they lean after a period of high winds. As a precaution in windy locations, place tall, very thin bamboo canes around the plant and tie green string loosely to "corset" the stems. No other care is needed, except to remove the spent blossoms and feed with compost or aged manure every year or two. In a "wild" situation, allow the spent flower spikes to go to seed and they will self-sow to produce even more of this delightful plant.

In most catalogs and garden books, this plant is usually called black cohosh, black snake-root, or bugbane—totally unflattering names for a highly desirable plant. "Fairy candles" is so much more appropriate and descriptive! This graceful eastern American native has found a home in woodlands and large borders around the world. When in flower it dominates any planting with its tall fairy wands of white blossoms. This large plant requires space, so plant it where it can spread, such as in a bed of hostas or ferns.

## where to grow

Fairy candles is at home in the center of a large island bed; at the back of a one-sided border; in a wild, woodland garden where it can spread freely; and as a tall feature in a bed of a ground cover such as pachysandra, periwinkle, ivy, or hosta. It likes part shade but will grow in full sun if ample moisture is provided. It isn't particularly fond of the heat and humidity of the Deep South.

### CIMICIFUGA RACEMOSA

**ZONES:** 3–9

**BLOOM TIME:** Mid- to late summer

**LIGHT:** Part shade

**HEIGHT:** 6–8 feet

**INTEREST:** Candles of long, elegant white flower spikes that tower above foliage

# LILY-OF-THE-VALLEY

## how to grow

Lily-of-the-valley is undemanding and tolerates almost any soil. For the best results, provide humus-rich soil and keep the plants well watered (not soggy) during the growing season. They are maintenance-free except for an occasional mulch with leaf compost or well-rotted manure in areas where the soil is lean.

No garden is complete without a bed of lily-of-the-valley to cut for the kitchen window-sill or bedside table. Many gardeners consider it indispensable for its uniquely fragrant flowers and broad, smooth green leaves of a very pleasant hue. In cool-climate gardens, it is a pleasingly invasive plant that likes to romp in the woods; it will spread until it reaches either a tree, rock, log, water, or other barrier. Once planted, it is hard to eliminate and will generally outlive the one who planted it by a century or two. To ensure blooms the first year (for a daughter's wedding, for example), make sure you buy pips (the under-ground stem with a dormant flower bud at the end) guaranteed to bloom the first year. Small nonflowering pips are often sold; these take a year or two to produce blooms.

## CONVALLARIA MAJALIS

**ZONES:** 2–8

**BLOOM TIME:** Mid- to late spring

**LIGHT:** Part shade

**HEIGHT:** 6–8 inches

**INTEREST:** Pure white bells of exquisitely fragrant flowers; handsome green foliage

## where to grow

Choose a location with care so your ancestors won't curse you for planting lily-of-the-valley "in the wrong place" because it has taken over in the garden. Plant it under shade trees and provide a barrier such as lawn edging to prevent invasive spreading.

Lily-of-the-valley is also a good seasonal indoor plant—even easier to force than spring bulbs. Special forcing varieties with extra-large pips are available to force in winter, providing delightful spring fragrance in a midwinter room. Transplant to the garden after danger of frost has passed.

# YELLOW CORYDALIS

## how to grow

Plant yellow corydalis in moist, woodsy soil. Water it, then forget it—until it flowers, of course. Maintenance? Nil. If you have an unusually dry summer, it will appreciate an occasional drink. Propagate from seeds—but instead of collecting the seeds and sowing them, just look around the parent plant for the bluish green seedlings that appear in spring. Transplant them to garden spots where you want long-lasting color, or give them to a friend whose garden needs a boost.

It's definitely worth getting down on your knees for a closer look at yellow corydalis. This charming plant has exquisite golden yellow flowers that bear a close resemblance to their kin, the bleeding heart. The blossoms are set off by lacy, fernlike grayish green leaves that add even more visual appeal. Since it has a proclivity for spreading freely with self-sown seedlings, yellow corydalis will happily form a colony as large as you allow. It shows up in paths, rock walls—even in chunks of dirt in your garden cart if you're not too faithful about emptying it. Call it weedy if you dare; a plant is only a weed if it grows in the wrong place—so just accept this delightful plant wherever it appears. If you insist on keeping it in bounds, look for clusters of bluish green seedlings in spring and hoe them down on a bright sunny morning.

## where to grow

Plant yellow corydalis along a woodland path or anywhere in a woodland garden where it can frolic freely. While it tolerates full sun in cool, moist climates, it does best in some shade. It doesn't handle desert climates or extreme heat well.

### CORYDALIS LUTEA

**ZONES:** 5–9

**BLOOM TIME:** Spring and summer

**LIGHT:** Part shade

**HEIGHT:** 12–15 inches

**INTEREST:** Grayish green, fernlike foliage with masses of golden yellow flowers from late spring to late summer

# UMBRELLA PLANT

## how to grow

Although it prefers to grow in wet, mucky soil, umbrella plant will grow in part shade in humus-rich soil that doesn't dry out. In full sun, it must have its feet in soil that is constantly wet—beside running or standing water. Water the plants well during drought conditions to keep them looking fresh. To propagate, use a pneumatic drill or excavator to chop off pieces of root after the frost has blackened the leaves in fall.

This highly ornamental foliage plant is not for the faint-hearted! Umbrella plant (also known as *Darmera*) is a Pacific Coast native with enormous leaves up to 18 inches across, on stalks that can reach 5 feet. It requires lots of space to grow, and in wet spots beside a stream, pond, or bog, it develops into a jungle that delights children. The leaves, which are edged in pointed scallops, are impressive in huge flower arrangements—they turn brilliant red in fall, another plus for this grand plant. The clusters of starry pink flowers show up on 3- to 5-foot stems before the foliage emerges.

## DARMERA PELTATA

**ZONES:** 5–9

**BLOOM TIME:** Early spring

**LIGHT:** Part shade

**HEIGHT:** 3–5 feet

**INTEREST:** Impressive large leaves that turn red in fall; pink flowers before the foliage appears

## where to grow

If you are fortunate enough to have a stream, pond, or bog, grow umbrella plant in the adjacent wet soil. If not, place it in humus-rich organic soil in a low spot where water collects after rain. It makes a noble sight when allowed to develop into large groups under tall trees.

# BLEEDING HEART

## how to grow

Like all bleeding hearts, 'Luxuriant' requires rich garden soil that doesn't dry out yet drains well. Increase your soil's drainage and moisture-holding capacity by digging in lots of organic matter. This plant requires little maintenance—mulch with leaf compost to retain moisture, but don't bury the crowns or they may rot.

As its name implies, 'Luxuriant' bleeding heart has heart-shaped blossoms, split at the bottom to show their paler inner petals. This shade-loving perennial is a hybrid of East and West Coast natives. The plant provides a summer-long display of beautiful reddish pink blossoms clustered atop 15-inch spikes. It is one of the longest blooming of all perennials. One of its most unusual characteristics likens this pretty plant to a mule—of all things. Since it never sets seeds (as a mule never bears a foal), it blooms profusely. This endless attempt to reproduce itself may be confusing to the plant, but gardeners consider it a real boon. Even without its never-ending blooms, 'Luxuriant' would be worth growing for its charming filigree foliage. It also makes an enchanting, long-lasting cut flower, allowing viewers to examine its intricate blossoms at their leisure.

## where to grow

'Luxuriant' is as happy in the transition zone between the sunny border and the woodland garden as it is in fairly deep shade. It doesn't like permanent shade at the north side of a building but is a great foundation plant at the northeast and northwest corners of buildings. It makes a superior ground cover, or use it in front of a border for its attractive foliage and constant color.

### DICENTRA X 'LUXURIANT'

**ZONES:** 3–9

**BLOOM TIME:** Summer

**LIGHT:** Part to deep shade

**HEIGHT:** 15 inches

**INTEREST:** Reddish pink heart-shaped blooms over lacy, fernlike foliage all season long

# FOXGLOVE

## how to grow

Foxglove requires rich, moist soil that doesn't dry out. The evergreen crowns resent standing water and may require winter protection (see page 117) in exposed northern areas. To increase your foxglove population, allow some spikes to produce seedpods. When stems turn brown, break open a few pods. If the seeds are brown, crush a few pods and shake the seeds onto moist, bare earth.

The common foxglove is native to Europe, but it has naturalized in many parts of the Northeast and Northwest. A large grove of these stately spires in bloom in a garden or along a roadside is a truly magnificent sight. Although a short-lived perennial, foxglove seeds itself freely in favorable conditions. Once established, colonies will regenerate themselves. Foxglove is easy to grow, and the sturdy flower stalks rise from low clumps of large leaves. The name "foxglove" is a corruption of "folks' glove," because the individual blossoms look like fingers cut from a glove. This plant, though toxic, has been used as a source of the powerful heart stimulant digitalis for over two hundred years.

## DIGITALIS PURPUREA

**ZONES:** 4–10

**BLOOM TIME:** Late spring to early summer

**LIGHT:** Part shade

**HEIGHT:** 4–5 feet

**INTEREST:** Tall, elegant pinkish purple or white flower spikes

## where to grow

Foxglove belongs scattered in shade gardens and along shady roadsides that aren't mowed until late summer. It can also be placed in more formal borders in the shade of large shrubs or small trees. It's perfectly at home in a shaded "wild" garden. Because it is tall and the foliage at the base can look somewhat tattered toward summer's end, locate foxglove behind shorter plants.

# LEOPARD'S BANE

## how to grow

Leopard's bane prefers light shade, but it will grow in full sun in rich soil that holds moisture well yet never gets waterlogged. Keep the plants well watered in early summer and mulch the soil around the roots, but avoid smothering the crowns, for this may cause them to rot out. In high temperatures, the plants have a tendency to go dormant in the middle of summer, so plant annuals or dahlias in front of leopard's bane to hide the bare earth.

Leopard's bane is the perennial equivalent of the springtime favorite forsythia. It bursts forth in all its golden glory in early spring to announce that winter is over and is one of the first daisies to bloom. Only the true English daisy and its offspring get a head start on this decorative plant. You'll find leopard's bane in flower when daffodils and bleeding hearts begin to bloom. The three together are a welcome sight after the dreary grays and browns of winter—especially in cold climates. Leopard's bane makes an excellent, long-lasting cut flower and looks terrific in a vase with the aforementioned spring-blooming companions. The Latin name, *Doronicum*, is derived from Arabic, and perhaps the common name, which doesn't appear to relate to anything familiar to temperate-climate gardeners, comes from a similar source.

## where to grow

Leopard's bane is just as happy naturalized in a woodland with wildflowers, hostas, and ferns as it is in a mixed border. In other words, it has that ability to look informal in natural settings and formal in more cultivated surroundings. Plant lots in a cutting garden for armfuls of daisies in early spring.

> ## DORONICUM CAUCASICUM
> **ZONES:** 4–9
> **BLOOM TIME:** Spring
> **LIGHT:** Part shade
> **HEIGHT:** 12–24 inches
> **INTEREST:** Golden yellow daisies in early spring; heart-shaped or triangular leaves

# LONGSPUR EPIMEDIUM

## how to grow

The key to success with longspur epimedium is soil preparation (as it is with almost every plant). It must have rich, organic soil that remains moist, but never stays wet. Once the plant is well established, it can tolerate some drought but will need watering during long dry spells. It requires only an annual trimming to ground level in early spring before new foliage starts to grow; reapply mulch at the same time.

This charming perennial represents an underused genus of rugged but delicate-looking plants with lovely flowers, very showy spring foliage, and a tough, no-nonsense ground-cover habit. The spurred blossoms sit like jewels atop 10- to 15-inch foliage that is pale bronze in spring and turns greener in summer. This is 'Lilafee'. Cut a few for a vase in the kitchen windowsill, where you can enjoy their delightful form up close for days.

## EPIMEDIUM GRANDIFLORUM

**ZONES:** 5–8

**BLOOM TIME:** Spring

**LIGHT:** Part shade

**HEIGHT:** 10–15 inches

**INTEREST:** Dainty white, yellow, and rose-violet blossoms atop pale bronze foliage

## where to grow

Epimedium is an extremely versatile plant in most shady situations. It is suitable for individual plantings in a rock garden or by a path at the foot of a tree. It's also perfect for use in large sweeps as a ground cover under trees or large shrubs, or as a foundation plant. Once plants fill in (which can take a while), they'll keep out most weeds. Epemedium is an unusual container plant for shady decks or patios, especially good for providing spring interest in combination with bulbs.

# SWEET WOODRUFF

## how to grow

Plant in well-drained, woodsy soil that retains moisture. Mulch thinly in early spring to maintain the organic content of the soil and hold in moisture. Provide water during long dry spells to keep the foliage from browning. Sweet woodruff requires no other care, not even cutting back. You can divide clumps to increase your supply at any time during the growing season. To keep it from spreading beyond a certain point, drive a sharp spade into the ground at the desired edge of the clump and pull up any runners beyond the cut boundary.

Sweet woodruff is a delightful little plant with soft green leaves the color of spring. The narrow leaves grow in a whorl (like the spokes of an umbrella) around square stems, creating a more delicate texture than most ground covers. The tiny white starlike blossoms sparkle above the foliage in spring and early summer and have a delicate fragrance. When crushed, this sweet-smelling plant has the scent of new-mown hay. (The aroma comes from coumarin, a chemical used by the perfume industry to help fix fragrances.) Added to wine, this herb creates that unique and delicious libation *Maibowle,* or spring wine. Sweet woodruff is a bewitching plant that makes a useful ground cover in shady locations, where it spreads freely and only rarely becomes a pest.

## where to grow

A shade garden without sweet woodruff is hardly worth contemplating. It will fit anywhere and everywhere, with wildflowers, with cultivated woodland treasures, or as a ground cover under shrubs and trees. As a ground cover, it mixes well with spring- or summer-flowering bulbs and lilies. Cut a few sprigs to accompany lily-of-the-valley in a dainty late-spring bouquet.

## GALIUM ODORATUM

**ZONES:** 4–9

**BLOOM TIME:** Spring and early summer

**LIGHT:** Part to full shade

**HEIGHT:** 4–9 inches

**INTEREST:** A useful ground cover with spring green leaves and twinkling white flowers

# BLOODY CRANESBILL

## how to grow

Bloody cranesbill prefers average garden soil. It is more tolerant of drought than other cranesbills and many other shade plants. It will also grow in moist soil, but not in areas where water stands. It requires little or no maintenance. To increase your supply, look for small seedlings near the parent plant in spring or dig up and divide clumps in early spring. Bloody cransesbill can tolerate western heat but not the heat and humidity of the Deep South.

The bloody cranesbill is a true perennial geranium (unlike the commonly grown red geranium more properly called *Pelargonium*). This geranium has an intense color that dominates its neighbors when in flower. It isn't to everyone's taste, but it makes a strong statement for gardeners who like bright colors. The leaves are small and lacy, produced in such numbers that the low-growing plants appear dense. The plant spreads to three to four times its height, making it an excellent choice for a ground cover. It also boasts a longer bloom time than most perennials.

## GERANIUM SANGUINEUM

**ZONES:** 4–7

**BLOOM TIME:** Summer

**LIGHT:** Part shade

**HEIGHT:** 10–15 inches

**INTEREST:** Intense reddish purple flowers; delicate mounds of lacy dark green foliage

## where to grow

Use this versatile geranium in almost any garden wherever a low-growing, colorful plant or delicate leaf texture is needed. Position it at the front of a border or at the edge of a woodland path. Because of its strong color, it is best planted beside foliage plants such as ferns, hostas, and Jack-in-the-pulpits, or alongside plants with white blossoms such as sweet woodruff, dwarf goat's beard, and foamflower. It blends well with the pale pink blossoms of its refined relative *G. sanguineum* var. *striatum*.

# HAKONE GRASS

## how to grow

Grow in consistently moist, well-drained soil. If a summer is particularly hot, the leaves can burn, so consistent moisture is especially important then.

Divide them every few years (especially if they start to die out in the center).

Chosen by the Perennial Plant Association as its plant of the year for 2009, Hakone grass, also known as Japanese forest grass, is a deciduous perennial grass with inconspicuous yellow-green flowers in midsummer and gracefully arching leaves.

## where to grow

Hakone grass is one of the few ornamental grasses that flourishes in shade. It works well as a ground cover in shady locations. It also does well in containers, in rock gardens, along pathways, and in mixed borders.

**HAKONECHLOA MACRA 'AUREOLA'**

**ZONES:** 5–9

**BLOOM TIME:** Mid- to late summer

**LIGHT:** Partial shade

**HEIGHT:** 12–18 inches

**INTEREST:** Graceful, arching, golden striped leaves

# LENTEN ROSE

## how to grow

Lenten rose is the easiest of the hellebore clan to grow. It thrives in less than ideal conditions, but flourishes best in soil rich in organic matter so that it holds moisture but never stays waterlogged. The plants will tolerate part and full shade, which makes them even more useful. They seed themselves freely unless you remove the spent blooms before the seedpods turn brown and burst open. In the North, the foliage remains attractive in winter only if sheltered from cold winds by hedges, solid fences, or woody evergreens (such as hemlock or mountain laurel).

Lenten rose is a wonderful ornamental plant that deserves a place in every shade garden the year round. The 2- to 4-inch-wide nodding blossoms come in a pleasing array of colors; some have spots inside the blooms. Because the showy parts of the flowers are the sepals instead of the petals, they remain attractive for weeks. The dark evergreen foliage is ornamental all year, especially in mild climates and when sheltered from icy winds in northern climates. Lenten rose is a tough plant that usually self-sows. When planted with different shades, it produces pleasing color variations.

## HELLEBORUS X HYBRIDUS

**ZONES:** 4–10

**BLOOM TIME:** Early spring

**LIGHT:** Part to full shade

**HEIGHT:** 18–24 inches

**INTEREST:** Pink, rosy purple, dark maroon, green, or white flowers; attractive evergreen foliage

## where to grow

Lenten rose loves shade—in woodland gardens, along garden pathways, and at building foundations. Use it by the house in place of overused traditional ground covers for long-lasting, glossy greenery. It also makes an excellent cut flower. Scatter seeds or transplant seedlings in the "back forty" to have extra plants for cutting.

# ALUMROOT

## how to grow

All coralbells require moist but well-drained organic soil that is rich and has close to neutral pH. Before planting, dig in lots of leaf compost. Where soils are naturally acidic, also dig in some dolomitic limestone to make them sweet. Mulch with leaf compost, keeping it away from the crowns to avoid encouraging rot. Water well during dry spells. The flowers of most of the varieties grown for foliage are not especially attractive and may be removed as soon as they appear. Divide in early spring to maintain vigor.

Coralbells is an easy-to-grow, rosy-flowered species. A cottage garden favorite, it is also the proud parent of many exciting new varieties hybridized in recent years. (*Heuchera sanguinea* is pictured here.) Its tiny coral-red blossoms wave on thin stems above lobed, kidney-shaped leaves. The foliage provides a pleasant background for the showy flower spikes and remains attractive all season.

## where to grow

Coralbells belong in both perennial borders and woodland gardens, in formal situations and informal plantings. To appreciate their wandlike blossoms, position them near the edge of the border or along a path or shady walkway. Although the blooms are held high, the thin stems are almost transparent, so they will not block the view of plants behind them. After bloom, the tidy clumps of foliage stay quite low to the ground.

### HEUCHERA

**ZONES:** 3–10

**BLOOM TIME:** Late spring and all summer

**LIGHT:** Part shade

**HEIGHT:** 12–18 inches

**INTEREST:** Coral-red flowers on thin, delicate-looking stems; attractive foliage

# PLANTAIN LILY

## how to grow

'Frances Williams' prefers light morning sun and afternoon shade, but will grow in almost full sun (except in the South) if given rich soil and constant moisture. Leaves will burn if given too much sun, but some bright, indirect light intensifies the variegation of the foliage and increases flowering. If you prefer foliage only, simply remove the flower stalks. Divide clumps only when they become overcrowded.

Hostas have become the perennial of choice for the shade garden, prized for their beautiful and richly textured foliage. No other plant is as attractive or as versatile in combination with other plants. Hostas are hands-down winners for their low-maintenance requirements and for their ability to outcompete weeds—not to mention for introducing more shades of blue and green foliage into the garden than any other plant! Colors range from forest green, chartreuse, and yellow to bluish green and grayish blue. Some cultivars are variegated at the leaf margins or with a central flame pattern in white, cream, or yellow. ('Krossa Regal' is pictured here.) Though sometimes overlooked, hosta blossoms make excellent cut flowers. Some varieties are exquisitely fragrant.

## HOSTA

**ZONES:** 3–9

**BLOOM TIME:** Early summer

**LIGHT:** Part shade

**HEIGHT:** 6–36 inches

**INTEREST:** Beautiful variegated leaves; white or pale lavender blossoms

## where to grow

Where rainfall is plentiful in summer, most landscapes in temperate climates have a site for this and other hostas. The lush foliage fits easily into shrub and perennial borders and is widely used as an accent among foundation plants, around the base of a tree, or scattered throughout low ground covers on banks or near lawns. In humid northern climates, you can grow fragrant hosta in full sun as long as the soil stays adequately moist. Where heavy soil is soggy from winter rains, plant on raised mounds for better drainage; the dormant crowns suffer from wet conditions.

# CRESTED IRIS

## how to grow

This tough little plant grows well in shade or full sun, if planted in rich, well-drained organic soil that doesn't stay too wet or too dry. When planting, don't cover the tops of the small rhizomes with soil or they will rot. Water well during dry spells. In a border, crested iris will soon outgrow its position, so divide it after a few years and place the surplus plants in the woods where they can wander at will. It is prey to slugs, which devour the delicate blooms like candy. (See page 114 for how to get rid of this pest.)

The crested iris is a choice dwarf that adapts well to cultivation. It has sparkling, sweetly scented 2-inch blossoms that vary from pale to deep lilac-blue, with darker blue and white markings and a yellow crest. Though short, the exquisite flowers show up remarkably well among the dwarf iris leaves. There are selections with dark blue or white flowers also with a yellow crest. This perennial makes a fine little ground cover—it spreads slowly but steadily, running along the ground with small creeping rhizomes. After it finishes blooming, it remains a tidy but dense forest of miniature iris leaves.

## where to grow

This dainty-looking yet rugged plant is equally happy in part to light shade; the more sun it gets, the more soil moisture it needs. Crested iris is a charming plant to place amid other wildflowers or beneath shrubs in a more formal mixed border. Try it too at the edge of a perennial border for late-spring color. It also deserves a spot in shady rock gardens.

## IRIS CRISTATA

**ZONES:** 3–9

**BLOOM TIME:** Spring

**LIGHT:** Part shade

**HEIGHT:** 4–8 inches

**INTEREST:** Delightful blue flowers on short plants; arching, soft, green leaves like large blades of grass

# SPOTTED DEAD NETTLE

## how to grow

Spotted dead nettle will grow in almost any soil type (but not wet) and any amount of shade. It does best in rich, well-mulched garden soil (keep the mulch away from the crown to avoid diseases). After flowering, shear the plants to produce a new flush of vigorous growth. In the South plants must be well watered and sheared occasionally to keep them looking tidy. Spotted dead nettle is easy to propagate; anytime you want to increase your supply, simply root stem cuttings or dig up rooted runners and replant.

Despite its rather unappealing colloquial name (it lacks the rash-producing hairs of the rather nasty stinging nettle), spotted dead nettle is a superior ground cover. It is dead easy to grow, it spreads without being invasive, and its purplish red flowers provide color all season long. Its small attractive green leaves are marked with a central band of silver-gray. There are also selections with silver-gray foliage edged in gray-green and others with showy pink, violet, or white flowers. In northern gardens, spotted dead nettle is one of the few plants that will tolerate dry shade.

## LAMIUM MACULATUM

**ZONES:** 4–10

**BLOOM TIME:** Late spring to summer

**LIGHT:** Part to full shade

**HEIGHT:** 12–15 inches

**INTEREST:** Colorful, very easy-to-grow ground cover

## where to grow

Grow spotted dead nettle wherever you need a ground cover—under trees or shrubs, along the edge of a shady driveway, with evergreen foundation plants, or to add color in shady areas. Plant it as a delicate textural contrast under large hostas, too. Since it tolerates dry shade better than most ground covers, spotted dead nettle can be used to replace sparse lawn under trees (and reduce your mowing chores).

# BIGLEAF GOLDENRAY

## how to grow

Bigleaf goldenray must have moist soil; otherwise it wilts dramatically and looks decidedly unhappy. If the location you have in mind is not naturally moist, add lots of organic matter such as leaf compost or peat moss to the soil before planting. Mulch with a thick layer of leaf compost, pine needles, or shredded pine bark, and water heavily during dry spells. Unfortunately, this plant loves the same moist, humus-rich conditions as slugs and snails, and these slimy pests can make inroads in the leaves. (To control slugs, see page 114.)

Bigleaf goldenray is a large, imposing plant with yellow to orange blossoms in flat-topped, well-branched clusters. It is grown partly for its huge, kidney-shaped leaves up to 20 inches wide; in some cultivars, the foliage is strikingly dark. ('Othello' is shown here.) The bright orange-yellow flower heads measure 2 to 5 inches across. It demands deep, moist soil that never dries out—conditions that can be difficult to find in parts of the Southeast and Southwest.

## where to grow

Place bigleaf goldenray to make a bold statement by a pond, alongside a stream, or at the edge of a swampy area. In constantly wet soil, this plant will grow in full sun; otherwise it must have part shade. Plant in combination with other vigorous foliage plants such as large-leafed hosta, umbrella plant, or giant butterbur. It is one of the few shade plants that offer yellow to orange flowers, so use it when you want to add this color to a planting scheme or to brighten an otherwise dark spot. Bigleaf goldenray is a bold plant in color and stature; it needs companion plants of similar size that are also vigorous growers so they won't be overwhelmed and overrun.

### LIGULARIA DENTATA

**ZONES:** 4–8

**BLOOM TIME:** Summer

**LIGHT:** Part shade

**HEIGHT:** 36–48 inches

**INTEREST:** Showy orange-yellow flowers; bold ornamental foliage

# LILYTURF

## how to grow

Lilyturf isn't too fussy about light conditions, but it definitely resents standing in water. Like spotted dead nettle (see page 182), it is one of the few plants that thrive in dry shade. Mow down the foliage in late winter or early spring just before the new leaves emerge to keep the plants looking fresh each spring. Where winters are mild, spring renewal may not be necessary if plants don't look tired or tattered. For more plants, divide established clumps in spring. Lilyturf is rarely troubled by diseases or pests—other than slugs and snails.

Lilyturf's tolerance for varying light conditions and its drought resistance makes it indispensable in the home landscape and for commercial plantings. It is a tough, problem-free, evergreen ground cover that remains attractive year round. Variegated selections, such as this 'Variegata', provide even more ornamental value. The flowers look like grape hyacinths and bloom pure white or in pale or deep shades of lilac-blue.

## LIRIOPE MUSCARI

**ZONES:** 6–10

**BLOOM TIME:** Late summer

**LIGHT:** Part shade

**HEIGHT:** 12–18 inches

**INTEREST:** Handsome evergreen ground cover with broad-leafed, grasslike foliage; lilac-blue or white blossoms

## where to grow

Plant lilyturf in shade or sun, wherever a tidy ground cover is desired. It looks its best when planted in large sweeps with different varieties swirled together. Its grasslike form looks equally good in urban courtyards, edging suburban entries, or in rural gardens. Variegated forms add significant garden interest, even when not in bloom.

# VIRGINIA BLUEBELLS

## how to grow

Virginia bluebells prefers humus-rich soil that retains moisture but is well drained. To optimize the soil for self-sowing, mulch well with leaf compost in late winter, before the new growth emerges.

To increase your planting, wait until the foliage has turned yellow, cut off the stems, and shake the plants over bare, humus-rich earth to scatter the seeds. The fleshy roots are brittle and are easily broken, so seeds are generally more successful than dividing. If relocation is necessary, the best time to do it is as the foliage goes dormant in late spring to early summer. Buy container-grown plants rather than collecting from the wild. They'll have a much better chance of survival and you won't disturb the natural plant community.

Virginia bluebells is a much-loved eastern native that produces clusters of nodding fragrant blossoms. Soft blue flowers begin as pink buds and often retain a faint blush of the bud color. A spring ephemeral, it blossoms in spring and goes dormant in the heat of summer. That means you need to plan for the hole it will leave behind. It is best combined with later-developing plants such as hostas, ferns, or shade-loving annuals; these will expand enough by midsummer to fill in the spaces left. Very easy to grow, it requires little or no maintenance. Keep it happy and it will self-sow freely, but never invasively.

## where to grow

To see Virginia bluebells dangling alongside a woodland path is one of the great joys of spring. Plant it also under trees or large shrubs. It looks at home combined with other native spring ephemerals such as violet, spring beauty, Mayapple, Eastern trout lily, and merrybells, as well as with "exotics" such as daffodil, bleeding heart, and leopard's bane.

**MERTENSIA VIRGINICA**

**ZONES:** 3–9

**BLOOM TIME:** Spring

**LIGHT:** Part to full shade

**HEIGHT:** 15–24 inches

**INTEREST:** Delightful blue flowers in spring; apple green foliage

# ALLEGHENY PACHYSANDRA

## how to grow

This pachysandra can grow in a range of soils, as long as it's not too dry and not in too much sun. It can be divided in the spring. When planting initially, plant 6 to 12 inches apart, as plants will fill in. They can be prone to leaf blight, so water with a soaker hose instead of a sprinkler, and don't let plants get overcrowded.

**This evergreen native to eastern North America is an alternative ground cover to the non-native English ivy and the invasive *Pachysandra terminalis*.**

### PACHYSANDRA PROCUMBENS

**ZONES:** 5–9

**BLOOM TIME:** Late spring

**LIGHT:** Partial shade to full shade

**HEIGHT:** 6–12 inches

**INTEREST:** Very small, fragrant white flowers on spikes before leaf-out in spring

## where to grow

Use Allegheny pachysandra as a ground cover in shady woodland gardens, in dappled shade under trees, and along walkways. It's a useful choice for a location that needs a deer-resistant and drought-resistant plant.

# WILD BLUE PHLOX

## how to grow

Provide wild blue phlox with slightly acidic, humus-rich soil that stays moist but well drained. After flowering and after the seeds have fallen (about 4 weeks after the blooms have ended), shear the plants to encourage new leaf growth. No other care is required. Divide established clumps if you wish to start new patches beyond the reach of self-sowing.

Wild blue phlox grows naturally from Quebec to Georgia, showing great adaptability to diverse climates. Its flower color varies from very pale blue to deep sky blue, with occasional purplish blue and pure white variations. The clusters of lightly fragrant flowers sit atop 12- to 15-inch stems of dark green foliage. The plant spreads slowly, but seeds itself to naturally increase the size of the planting. The offspring are frequently a different shade than the parent plant. Wild blue phlox makes itself at home in woodland gardens and spreads to shady locations with conditions it finds comfortable.

## where to grow

Grow wild blue phlox in woodland gardens, especially along paths, with other spring-flowering wildflowers. It works well as a mild-mannered flowering ground cover, because it will not overrun its neighbors. Give it room to spread itself around and it will produce delightful color combinations, popping up in the most unexpected places—even in mulched paths. Plant extra for cutting—it's beautiful in a vase.

### PHLOX DIVARICATA

**ZONES:** 3–9

**BLOOM TIME:** Spring

**LIGHT:** Part shade

**HEIGHT:** 12–15 inches

**INTEREST:** Charming, fragrant blue flowers

# MAYAPPLE

## how to grow

Mayapple prefers rich, moist organic soil. On sites that do not offer evenly moist soil, it needs to be mulched heavily with leaf compost or chopped leaves and watered in dry weather. Otherwise, this plant is maintenance-free. Create new plantings by digging up pieces of the plant as it goes dormant and transplanting to the desired new location.

Mayapple is native to the woods of eastern and southern North America and provides a different look in ground covers for shade. When young, the plants develop only one large (1 foot across), shiny green, umbrella-like leaf. As it matures, Mayapple develops a pair of large leaves on a 15- to 18-inch stem. Its nodding, 2-inch-wide solitary white blossom appears at the fork between the two leaves. Later, the plant develops a large, yellow, egg-shaped edible fruit that can be used to make jams and jellies. Unless you're looking for them, it's easy to miss the flowers and fruits of Mayapple since they're tucked away under the pair of leaves.

### PODOPHYLLUM PELTATUM

**ZONES:** 3–9

**BLOOM TIME:** Spring to early summer

**LIGHT:** Part shade

**HEIGHT:** 15–18 inches

**INTEREST:** Handsome native plant with large leaves, white flowers, and edible yellow fruits

**CAUTION:** Although the leaves and roots have medicinal properties, they are very poisonous if eaten in large quantities.

## where to grow

Mayapple is a woodland wildflower and grows best in sites that mimic its natural home. The ideal location for Mayapple is on a moist bank or a raised knoll in the woodland garden so that the nodding white flowers and yellow fruits can be seen more easily. Use it as a ground cover under tall trees or beside large shrubs, and interplant it with other vigorous growers to create a tapestry of textures. In the far North, it will grow in full sun if the soil remains constantly moist but not waterlogged. Mayapple's underground shoots ramble to form large colonies—so give it lots of room.

# JACOB'S LADDER

## how to grow

Jacob's ladder tends to be a short-lived perennial, but it usually self-sows to replace itself. It needs only average garden or woodsy soil that doesn't get too dry or too wet. Remove the flower spikes after the seedpods have turned brown. To ensure replacement plants, shake pods around the original plant or in new areas to scatter the seeds. Watch out for seedlings the following spring; they quickly develop the characteristic laddered foliage. Thin the seedlings so they don't crowd out each other.

Jacob's ladder is a European native whose colloquial name originated from the leaves that resemble the ladder in Jacob's dream in the book of Genesis 28:12. It is a free-flowering perennial that blooms in late spring and early summer with 1-inch blue or white blossoms on upright stems. The bright green, fernlike foliage remains attractive after the plant has flowered. It has an American cousin, creeping Jacob's ladder (*P. reptans*), which is longer-lived in the garden than its European counterpart; its spreading 8- to 15-inch stems produce masses of twinkling lavender-blue flowers.

## where to grow

Jacob's ladder is useful in any woodland setting as well as in a mixed border. So that the entire plant may be seen and appreciated to its fullest, don't crowd it with other plants. It is ideal planted with shorter-growing plants so that the Jacob's ladder flower spikes stand well above its neighbors. It may not thrive in really hot summers.

## POLEMONIUM CAERULEUM

**ZONES:** 3–9

**BLOOM TIME:** Late spring to early summer

**LIGHT:** Part shade

**HEIGHT:** 18–24 inches

**INTEREST:** Airy spikes of bright blue or white flowers and attractive fernlike foliage

# VARIEGATED SOLOMON'S SEAL

## how to grow

Variegated Solomon's seal requires a rich, woodsy soil; though it tolerates dryness, it grows best in soil that stays relatively moist, but never water-logged. Incorporate lots of leaf compost or other organic matter before planting. After planting, keep the soil mulched to conserve moisture and suppress weeds. Water plantings during dry spells. To start new plants, dig up portions of the plants with a sharp spade in fall, after the foliage has been touched by frost. Alternatively, mark the location of plants in fall and transplant in spring before they break dormancy and poke above the ground.

The showy leaves of variegated Solomon's seal are bright green, edged in white. This coloration makes a shady spot positively sparkle all season long. Like other Solomon's seals, this variety has graceful, arching, unbranched stems; pairs of 1-inch white flowers hang down from the axils of the leaves. The flowers have a fragrance that is particularly delightful on warm, calm evenings.

## POLYGONATUM ODORATUM 'VARIEGATUM'

**ZONES:** 4–9

**BLOOM TIME:** Spring and early summer

**LIGHT:** Part shade

**HEIGHT:** 18–24 inches

**INTEREST:** Arching stems with fragrant white flowers and attractive white-variegated foliage

## where to grow

This plant is attractive and useful for adding elegance to shady locales—especially when planted amid a ground cover such as hosta, pachysandra, or periwinkle. Its elegant, arching stems provide a very pleasing contrast to the lower-growing plants. Touches of white on the leaves provide the added dimension of color contrast in a swath of shady greens. Plant some near a path so that its sweet fragrance can be readily enjoyed.

# JAPANESE PRIMROSE

## how to grow

This colorful plant must have rich, slightly acidic moist to wet soil that never dries out. Japanese primrose will even grow in running water that completely covers the plant for short periods. It self-sows freely to produce dense groups. It can be grown in ordinary woodland conditions but it must be well watered during any drought. Buy nursery starts or plant from seeds.

The Japanese primrose is one of the easiest to grow members of this large but sometimes fussy genus. It produces beautiful, colorful flowers. In the moist to wet conditions that it prefers, the Japanese primrose will grow into a vigorous clump with several 18- to 24-inch flower stems. Its characteristic whorls of flowers are tiered like candelabras and appear in shades of carmine or crimson-red, pink, and white. The plants cross-pollinate freely to produce seedlings of intermediate shades—with dark red being the dominant hue.

## where to grow

If given room, this primrose naturalizes readily to form large clumps. Japanese primrose loves wet feet, so choose a home for it in any area that stays moist or wet. Good locations include beside or in shallow water, a stream, bog, pond, or just a low spot where water regularly collects after rain. In northern climates, it will grow in full sun if the soil is constantly wet. If there is a damp or wet spot in your garden, don't deprive yourself of this colorful display.

## PRIMULA JAPONICA

**ZONES:** 5–8

**BLOOM TIME:** Late spring to early summer

**LIGHT:** Part shade

**HEIGHT:** 18–24 inches

**INTEREST:** Showy whorls of colorful flowers for several weeks

# POLYANTHA PRIMROSE

## how to grow

Plant primroses in rich, slightly acidic soil, fortified with plenty of organic matter and kept moist during the spring growth spurt and bloom periods. Though they'll survive with less water in summer and fall, polyantha primroses do best in moist soil. You can help keep the ground moist and cool by mulching well with compost or another organic material. Divide crowded clumps after flowering in spring or in early autumn. If you notice snail or slug damage, go out on an early-morning foray and pluck off these munching pests. (Also see page 114.)

Polyantha primroses are a popular group of hybrids that have evolved from repeated crossings of several genera, including *P. elatior*, *P. juliae*, and *P. vulgaris* (the English primrose). They form tight, low clumps of crinkled and deeply veined leaves; many are evergreen but others die back in winter. All are glorious in full bloom, lighting up shadowy areas with their cheery flower clusters in radiant colors. Few other plants embody the essence of spring with the verve and gaiety of the polyantha primrose.

## PRIMULA X POLYANTHA

**ZONES:** 5–8

**BLOOM TIME:** Early to late spring

**LIGHT:** Filtered shade

**HEIGHT:** 6–12 inches

**INTEREST:** Multicolored blossoms with contrasting yellow eyes; easy to grow in moist, semi-shaded locations

## where to grow

The polyanthas are perfect primroses for beds in semishaded lawns, glorious either in formal masses or in small colonies. They tuck easily into rock gardens and are ideal in wide, shallow pots on covered patios and decks. The polyanthas are excellent edging plants along perennial borders in part sun, bursting into flower while late bloomers are just getting started with spring growth. When background plants mature later in the season, they shield the primroses from harsh summer sun.

# SPOTTED LUNGWORT

## how to grow

Spotted lungwort will grow in ordinary soil. For the foliage to remain good looking all summer, it must be grown in a shady location in rich, organic soil that never dries out yet never stays too wet. Some varieties are susceptible to powdery mildew; this fungal disease is more noticeable on plants that have been stressed from growing in conditions that are too wet or too dry. To increase the size of your planting, divide the crowns carefully as soon as the flowers are past their peak. Plant divisions in good rich soil and water thoroughly as the new leaves emerge.

Spotted lungwort provides two seasons of interest. It starts in spring with pink, blue, or white trumpet-shaped flowers on 10- to 12-inch stems. These are followed by showy green foliage that is spotted silver-gray; in some newer selections, the entire leaf may be silver-gray. The pink- and blue-flowered varieties often open as one color (pink) and turn to the other (blue) as they mature. Lungwort is so named because its leaves are said to look like a diseased lung. 'Mrs. Moon' is shown here.

## where to grow

Plant spotted lungwort under the high shade of tall trees or large shrubs. It looks most at home when interplanted with native wildflowers and spring-flowering bulbs. Lungwort's showy foliage provides a long season of interest when planted alongside ground covers such as pachysandra that are solid green, or those that flower in early spring and are green for the rest of the year, such as periwinkle.

## PULMONARIA SACCHARATA

**ZONES:** 3–9

**BLOOM TIME:** Spring

**LIGHT:** Part shade

**HEIGHT:** 10–12 inches

**INTEREST:** Colorful flowers followed by ornamental spotted foliage that remains attractive all summer long

# FEATHERLEAF RODGERSIA

## how to grow

Featherleaf rodgersia requires humus-rich soil that remains constantly moist, but it does not like standing water. It resents drying out, which will cause leaves (or leaf edges) to turn brown. To promote even soil moisture, mulch heavily and water thoroughly during dry spells. In northern climates, it will tolerate full sun if grown in damp soil near a stream, pond, or bog; it appreciates winter protection wherever snow cover is unreliable. Featherleaf rodgersia will survive in many parts of Zone 4 if given winter protection.

Featherleaf rodgersia produces lovely plumes of 3- to 4-foot well-branched flower spikes of rose-red with a multitude of tiny flowers that together produce lots of color. These are set off by very beautiful bronze foliage that is similar to a horse chestnut leaf, with its broad leaflets arranged like the fingers of a hand. This plant is a large, shade-loving perennial from the Orient that provides a flourish of color in late spring and early summer. Its highly ornamental foliage provides a distinctive accent to the woodland or formal shady garden for the remainder of the growing season.

## RODGERSIA PINNATA

**ZONES:** 5–9

**BLOOM TIME:** Late spring to early summer

**LIGHT:** Part shade

**HEIGHT:** 36–48 inches

**INTEREST:** Showy rose-red flowers and large, attractive bronze leaves

## where to grow

This plant looks best when featured as an accent plant amid one or more low-growing ground covers in a shade border or woodland garden. Even when not in bloom, its big leaves add architectural interest to any planting. It can also be used in combination with other bold-leafed plants such as umbrella plant, large-leafed hostas, bigleaf goldenray, giant butterbur, and tall ferns. This produces a feeling of the tropics in a temperate climate.

# BLOODROOT

## how to grow

Choose a spot with part shade and rich, woodsy soil that retains moisture, but is well drained. Place the thick bloodroot rhizomes horizontally and 1 inch deep in soil. Add lots of organic matter before planting. Mulch annually with chopped leaves or compost in fall after the foliage has died down. Water thoroughly in dry conditions to prevent the foliage from going dormant and disappearing. Divide the rhizomes in late summer when the leaves turn yellow. Bloodroot spreads both by the rhizomes and from self-sown seedlings to form a moderately large colony.

Bloodroot is one of the joys of spring in the woods of eastern North America. It emerges from the ground with leaves wrapped around the bud; the leaves unroll as the flowers open. The 2-inch-wide, purest white blossoms open early, with the flowers each having eight or more petals. Sadly, they remain open but a few days. The lovely blooms are followed by highly distinctive gray-green lobed foliage that remains attractive for most of the summer, making an interesting and unusual ground cover. Both scientific and common names are derived from the blood-red sap that is produced by the thick, fleshy rhizomes. It was used by some Native Americans as a dye for clothing and as body paint.

## where to grow

Many agree that no woodland garden is complete without a large patch of bloodroot. Plant it toward the front of a formal shade garden for spring and summer beauty. Or sprinkle plants along the edge of a path in a shady bower. Use it for a ground cover under deciduous shrubs; mix several patches among other not-too-aggressive ground covers (such as Allegheny spurge or European ginger) to cover large areas beneath deciduous trees.

## SANGUINARIA CANADENSIS

**ZONES:** 3–9

**BLOOM TIME:** Early spring

**LIGHT:** Part shade

**HEIGHT:** 4–8 inches

**INTEREST:** Starry white flowers and beautiful gray-green leaves that form a pleasing ground cover

**CAUTION:** Bloodroot rhizomes are toxic—don't eat them!

# FALSE SOLOMON'S SEAL

## how to grow

As with other native woodland plants, false Solomon's seal is happiest in light shade and slightly acidic soil that's rich in organic matter. However, it isn't too fussy as long as the soil remains somewhat moist (not wet) during the growing season. It tolerates competition from surface tree roots better than many shade plants. The best time to divide and transplant is when the plants go dormant in late summer. New plants can also be produced from seeds collected from the ripe fruits in late summer.

False Solomon's seal is native to North America and has found its way into many woodland gardens across the country. In spring and early summer, each 2- to 3-foot stem is tipped with a plumelike cluster of fragrant, starlike creamy white flowers. These are followed by green berries that ripen to a speckled pinkish red. The unbranched stems arch gracefully and have wide, bright green leaves arrayed along the sides. The foliage remains ornamental all summer long. Plants spread slowly to produce handsome groups; it must know it looks its best in large patches.

## SMILACINA RACEMOSA

**ZONES:** 3–9

**BLOOM TIME:** Spring to early summer

**LIGHT:** Part shade

**HEIGHT:** 24–36 inches

**INTEREST:** Elegant, arching stems with bright green foliage and fragrant, creamy white flowers at the tips

## where to grow

False Solomon's seal blends well with hosta, rodgersia, globeflower, and native wildflowers such as ladybells. Use it to add a graceful note to a massed planting of low ground covers, or in groups to replace lawn around tree trunks. To enjoy its sweet fragrance, plant near an often-used path.

# CELANDINE POPPY

## how to grow

Celandine poppy is easy to grow in woodsy soil that doesn't dry out. If allowed to dry out in the summer, it will survive, but the foliage will disappear as plants go dormant. Mulch around the plants and water well during rainless spells. It self-sows freely to produce lots of new plants—if you don't want seedlings, deadhead to prevent this. Little other care is required, and it is relatively pest-free. The plants may be moved to new locations when they are very small, but they are best left undisturbed once established because of their brittle, fleshy roots.

Celandine poppy, also called wood poppy, is a beautiful native of eastern North America. It produces 3- to 4-inch butter yellow, upward-facing flowers similar to those of the Welsh poppy. The highly ornamental, deeply lobed blue-green foliage has a matte surface very similar to bloodroot—the pair make delightful companions. Celandine poppy is a not-too-fussy low-maintenance plant that self-sows, spreading freely but not invasively to form large colonies. Stems produce a bright orange-yellow sap that was used by Native Americans to make a natural dye.

## where to grow

With the delightful habit of popping up in unexpected places to compose interesting combinations of color, texture, and form, celandine poppy is most at home in woodland gardens where it can romp at will. The plants add delightful visual appeal when interplanted with spring-flowering bulbs such as Spanish bluebells, grape hyacinth, and camassia.

**a word of caution:** Don't confuse this plant with another related celandine, *Chelidonium majus*. Though they are related and the leaves of both look quite similar, this celandine has a much smaller flower and a problematic, weedy disposition.

### STYLOPHORUM DIPHYLLUM

**ZONES:** 4–9

**BLOOM TIME:** Spring and early summer

**LIGHT:** Part shade

**HEIGHT:** 12–18 inches

**INTEREST:** Brilliant butter yellow flowers above attractive blue-green foliage

# MEADOW RUE

## how to grow

In the North, meadow rue can be grown in full sun, providing the soil is rich, well-drained loam that stays evenly moist. In the South, it requires the same soil conditions but can only be grown in part shade. (It does not handle the dry heat of the Southwest very well.) Once established, the very strong, thick-stemmed plants rarely need staking and should be left undisturbed. Divide plants in spring only to increase your supply. They are surprisingly narrow (and delicate) for their height; plants should be spaced only 18 inches apart for the best effect.

Meadow rue is a sensational perennial, a tall plant that is remarkably delicate and graceful in appearance. The summer-to-fall visual feast begins with lacy, columbine-like, blue-green foliage that appears on windproof purple stems. This is followed by a cloud of lavender to purple blossoms that appear in a large, well-branched spray above the towering stems. *Thalictrum acquilegiifolum* is shown here.

## THALICTRUM

**ZONES:** 4–9

**BLOOM TIME:** Late summer to early fall

**LIGHT:** Part shade to full sun

**HEIGHT:** 6–8 feet

**INTEREST:** Very tall and incredibly elegant stems with beautiful blue-green foliage; topped with a mist of lavender flowers

## where to grow

Meadow rue is a choice plant that can stand on its own in large beds. It is more commonly mixed in with other plants to act as a towering accent above its neighbors. It's an obvious back-of-the-border plant, but try it in the middle of a border too, for the plants behind it can still be seen through its delicate floral display.

# FOAMFLOWER

## how to grow

Foamflower is a tough little plant; it isn't bothered by pests and requires little care to keep it growing and flowering. Like most other native woodland species, foamflower is happiest in rich, organic soil that never dries out and never stays soggy. Before planting, incorporate lots of organic matter into the soil; also mulch with compost or chopped leaves every year in late fall or early spring to maintain a high humus level. Dig up and divide the plants in early spring before they begin flowering or in the early summer after flowering. (Water well afterward and shade with newspaper.) You can also divide foamflower in fall.

Foamflower is a pretty ground cover with starry white flowers that have a noticeable pink blush—especially apparent as the blossoms age. The pale green, evergreen foliage is delightfully veined with burgundy; in winter and when grown in only part shade, the entire leaf usually turns bronze-burgundy. This easy-to-grow, spreading species carpets the ground with a dense mat and grows well at the base of shrubs and other tall plants. Foamflower adapts well to diverse areas and sites. In recent years, new, larger selections with highly ornamental foliage have been developed.

## where to grow

Grow foamflower as a delicately textured ground cover in shady sites under trees, shrubs, or other tall perennials. It blends well with most plants and looks especially attractive with spring-flowering bulbs poking through its mat. It is particularly useful for covering large areas; in the right conditions it spreads freely and quickly.

### TIARELLA CORDIFOLIA

**ZONES:** 3–9

**BLOOM TIME:** Spring

**LIGHT:** Part to full shade

**HEIGHT:** 6–12 inches

**INTEREST:** Masses of frothy white flowers, tinged in pink; attractive, pale green foliage with burgundy veins; a tough ground cover

# SPIDERWORT

### how to grow

Most spiderworts need moist, well-drained acidic soil. Pruning to 8 to 12 inches after flowering can produce a second blooming and also prevents them from going to seed and spreading too aggressively. They may go dormant in dry soils in the summer, especially in the South. When they flourish, it's helpful to divide the plants every few years.

*Tradescantia* is long-blooming and resilient, and there are many varieties available.

## TRADESCANTIA

**ZONES:** 4–9

**BLOOM TIME:** Early to midsummer

**LIGHT:** Partial shade

**HEIGHT:** 1–3 feet

**INTEREST:** Flowers that are usually bluish purple but can also be white, pink, or red

### where to grow

Use spiderwort in borders, edging, woodland gardens, and even in containers. It pairs well with coreopsis and lady's mantle.

# TOAD LILY

## how to grow

Toad lily requires the same conditions as Solomon's seal and many other shade plants—rich, woodsy soil that never dries out, but never floods. Incorporate lots of leaf compost before planting, keep the soil mulched, and water well during drought. Divide plants in early spring before they break dormancy. Don't cut down the leaves in fall; that will make it easy to find them in spring to divide for more plants.

Despite its unflattering name, toad lily is a charming Asian plant that flowers late in the year when there isn't much color in the shade garden. The 1-inch blossoms must be seen up close to be fully appreciated. They have six white petals (tepals, technically), spotted in purple and maroon. Their six-part stamens protrude from the flower in a very interesting arrangement. Flowers grow in a row like a chain of orchids draped along the stem. With leaves arranged on either side of an unbranched but elegantly arched stem, the foliage resembles that of Solomon's seal.

## where to grow

Grow toad lily in shady areas where color is needed toward the end of the gardening season. It blends in well with other plants, but to enjoy it to its fullest, plant it at the edge of the border or beside a path where the remarkable flowers can easily be seen up close. Plant enough so you can cut a few to bring inside, for these make good (and fascinating) cut flowers. Underplanting with autumn crocus (*Colchicum autumnale*) makes a really striking combination.

### TRICYRTIS HIRTA

**ZONES:** 5–9

**BLOOM TIME:** Late summer to fall

**LIGHT:** Part shade

**HEIGHT:** 24–36 inches

**INTEREST:** Fascinating flowers on plants resembling Solomon's seal

# HYBRID GLOBEFLOWER

## how to grow

Globeflower grows well in moist to wet soil, as along the edge of a stream, pond, or bog. It also thrives in a border that has heavy loam, rich in organic matter. Take care to keep roots moist; plants will go dormant if allowed to dry out in the summer. However, globeflower resents the humidity and heat of the Deep South. (It does not grow well in the Southwest, either.) Deadheading will prolong the flowering period. Propagate by division in fall, but to increase your plantings it is better to buy new plants, because clumps produce the most spectacular display if they are left undivided.

Globeflower is an elegant flower for the shade garden. The solitary flowers, shaped like oversized buttercups, sit atop 24- to 36-inch stems. Blossoms of cream, sunny yellow, or rich orange appear in late spring or early summer; some selections produce a second flush of flowers in the late summer or early fall. Its clumps of deeply cleft leaves are attractive all season long. The hybrid forms, indicated by the x in the botanical name, involve several species; all have larger flowers than the wild species. Globeflower is a long-lasting cut flower for spring and early-summer arrangements.

### TROLLIUS X CULTORUM

**ZONES:** 4-7

**BLOOM TIME:** Late spring to early summer

**LIGHT:** Part shade to full sun

**HEIGHT:** 24–36 inches

**INTEREST:** Globe-shaped flowers in cream, orange, or yellow over large, divided green leaves

## where to grow

Globeflower is suitable for any shade garden. It can be planted with native ferns and wildflowers or mixed with other imported exotics. All shades are pleasing with deep blue flowers such as those of Siberian irises or lupines.

# MERRYBELLS

## how to grow

Merrybells prefer rich, well-drained organic soil that stays evenly moist. Therefore, apply mulch in late winter and keep the plants well watered—especially in early summer. Feeding in spring with a balanced fertilizer encourages more vigorous growth and a better floral display. No other care is required.

This small eastern and central North American native is a sweet plant that never fails to impress—if you take time to notice the flowers. The delicate, bell-shaped, 1- to 1½-inch-long yellow blossoms of merrybells hang down. It is easy to pass them by without a glance because they pull down the tips of the stems. The foliage, resembling a smaller version of Solomon's seal, remains attractive all season. Merrybells spread with underground shoots but they are noninvasive.

## where to grow

Merrybells flower early with other spring ephemerals and combine well with other native woodland wildflowers and spring-flowering bulbs, such as daffodils and Spanish bluebells. They belong in a woodland garden with other small plants. They also show off well in front of evergreen shrubs such as rhododendron and mountain laurel, where the beautiful blossoms can stand out against dark foliage.

**UVULARIA GRANDIFLORA**

**ZONES:** 3–9

**BLOOM TIME:** Spring

**LIGHT:** Part shade

**HEIGHT:** 12–18 inches

**INTEREST:** Charming yellow flowers on a small, graceful plant

# TUFTED VIOLET

## how to grow

Tufted violet requires evenly moist soil that never dries out and never floods. In these conditions, it will grow in part shade or even in full sun where summers are cool in the North. In the South, it despairs of the July and August heat and humidity; shear plants back and wait for fall for a second show. Mulch in late winter to retain moisture, but avoid smothering the crowns, which may cause the plants to rot. Deadhead to keep the plants looking fresh and produce more flowers. Tufted violet grows readily from seeds, but it can also be propagated from cuttings.

For sheer abundance of flowers, few perennials come close to producing the number of blossoms (for as long) as the tufted violet. Flowering begins in early summer and continues until hard frost cuts plants down. This plant shrugs off light frosts. Blossoms of tufted violet are 1 to 1½ inches in diameter and often have a light fragrance. Selections are usually of one color and some feature a contrasting eye. They are usually compact growers that spread two to three times as wide as they are tall. Tufted violet is easy to grow and requires little maintenance.

## VIOLA CORNUTA

**ZONES:** 5–9

**BLOOM TIME:** Summer to fall

**LIGHT:** Part shade

**HEIGHT:** 8–10 inches

**INTEREST:** Masses of small, pansy-like flowers from early summer until fall

## where to grow

Grow large groups of tufted violet wherever you want long-lasting splashes of color. It can be used as a ground cover under trees and shrubs. It also provides summer color amid wildflowers and flowering bulbs that have their spring fling and then take the rest of the year off. This plant is a superb perennial for patio containers and window boxes, because it flowers for such a long period with little care. Pot some up for the kitchen windowsill—they're sure to bring more than a few smiles.

# APPALACHIAN BARREN STRAWBERRY

## how to grow

Though it is most successful in slightly acidic, humus-rich soil, barren strawberry can tolerate a variety of well-drained soil types. Once the plant is established, it can tolerate periods of drought, but it won't do well in the hot, humid South. This plant is generally free of pests.

Native to eastern North America, this strawberry is strictly ornamental, despite the leaves' resemblance to plants that produce sweet—edible—fruit. In a spot where a ground cover is needed, this is a good alternative to pachysandra, which can be invasive.

## where to grow

Use for massing (in sunnier locations), as a ground cover, or underplanted in a perennial garden. Seeds can be sown directly outdoors in fall or spring; established plants send out runners and fill in empty spaces.

### WALDSTEINIA FRAGARIOIDES

**ZONES:** 4–7

**BLOOM TIME:** Spring

**LIGHT:** Part shade

**HEIGHT:** 4–8 inches

**INTEREST:** Foliage that turns bronze in winter and dainty yellow spring flowers

# GLOSSARY

**ACCENT PLANT:** A plant that draws attention by its extraordinary display.

**ACIDIC SOIL:** Soil with a pH value of less than 7.0.

**ALKALINE SOIL:** Soil with a pH value of more than 7.0.

**BIENNIAL:** A plant that grows vegetatively one year; flowers, fruits, and seeds the next; and then dies.

**BORDER:** A garden bed that is designed to edge or frame something, often backed by a wall, hedge, or fence.

**BRACT:** A colorful, leaflike structure that appears below a flower, such as the showy part of a dogwood or poinsettia "flower."

**BRUSHWOOD:** Twigs cut in late winter to use for staking plants. Birch twigs are ideal.

**CLUMP:** Stems or underground shoots with several vegetative buds.

**COTTAGE GARDEN:** Garden based on an English style of gardening in which many plants are placed in a dense and seemingly random fashion.

**CROSS-POLLINATE:** When a flower of one plant is fertilized by the pollen from a flower of another plant.

**CROWN:** The part of a plant where the roots are attached to the shoots.

**CULTIVATION:** To work the soil by digging, forking, hoeing, or using a mechanical device.

**CUTTING GARDEN:** A bed for growing flowers to harvest.

**DEADHEADING:** The removal of spent flowers to tidy up a plant and force it to put its energy into producing more flowers instead of seeds.

**DIVISION:** A method of propagation in which the crown of a plant is divided into two or more pieces.

**DOUBLE-FLOWERED:** A flower with more than the usual number of petals.

**EPHEMERAL:** A plant that has a very short growth cycle.

**EYE:** A ring of a deeper or paler color around the center of the flower; for example, many garden phlox and some dianthus have eye rings.

**FLORET:** A small flower that makes up part of a large flower head.

**FLOWER HEAD:** A flower composed of many small flowers.

**FLUSH:** Abundant new growth produced after dormancy or being cut back.

**FOUNDATION PLANT:** A plant placed next to a building to hide the foundation and soften the hard architectural lines.

**GENUS:** A group of closely related species.

**GROUND COVER:** Plants that are used to cover bare ground; they usually spread to form dense colonies that choke out weeds.

**HUMUS:** Dark, fine-textured material that results from organic material reaching an advanced stage of decay.

**HYBRID:** A plant that results from cross-pollination of genetically dissimilar plants.

**INFLORESCENCE:** The flowering part of a plant.

**INTERPLANT:** To place plants between other plants to extend seasonal interest—such as planting spring bulbs among plants that develop later, such as hosta.

**ISLAND BED:** A flower bed that you can walk around.

**LEAF COMPOST:** Organic matter made from leaves that have been allowed to decay. Also called leaf mold.

**LIMESTONE:** A soil amendment containing calcium; it slowly raises the pH of a soil so it is more alkaline (basic). Dolomitic limestone is the safest form to use. If soil tests indicate adequate magnesium, then calcitic limestone is the safest form to use.

**MEADOW GARDENING:** Growing plants in an open area resembling an uncultivated field. Undesirable species are cut back or eliminated.

**MULCH:** A layer of organic or inorganic material placed around plants to hold in moisture and reduce weeds.

**PINCHING:** Snipping out (or using fingernails to literally pinch out) the growing point of a plant to promote fullness and bushiness.

**POWDERY MILDEW:** A disease that coats the upper surface of leaves and flowers with a pale gray or white dustlike growth.

**PROPAGATE:** To create new plants.

**RAISED BED:** A bed that is higher than the surrounding area, often contained within a low retaining wall composed of rocks, bricks, logs, or boards.

**RECURRENT BLOOM (REPEAT BLOOMING):** Blooming after the main flush of flowers has passed.

**SEMIDOUBLE:** A flower with two or three rows of petals.

**SEMIWOODY:** A perennial that has shrublike stems.

**SEPAL:** The usually green part of many flowers that encloses the petals and reproductive organs.

**SINGLE-FLOWERED:** A flower with a single row of petals.

**SPECIES:** A group of plants within a genus that are more or less identical.

**SPIKE:** A long, usually unbranched flower stem.

**STAMEN:** The male reproductive organ in a flower where pollen is produced.

**STEM CUTTINGS:** Pieces of shoots cut from a plant to create new plants.

**TEPAL:** Parts of a flower that are not petals or sepals, but look like them; for example, the showy parts of tulip flowers are tepals.

**TRANSPLANT:** To dig up and relocate a plant.

**TRUE TO VARIETY:** The condition in which a plant's seedling offspring are identical in appearance to the parent plant.

**UNDERPLANT:** To plant flowers or bulbs beneath the canopy of a larger plant to add color to the garden without taking up additional space.

**VARIEGATED LEAVES:** Leaves that are patterned in a different color.

**VARIETY:** A subdivision of a species; commonly used in place of the horticultural term *cultivar*, which is a cultivated variety.

**WELL-DRAINED SOIL:** Soil that drains quickly, even after heavy rain.

**WET FEET:** The condition in which a plant is sitting in waterlogged soil.

**WHORL:** A circle of three or more leaves or flowers around a plant stem.

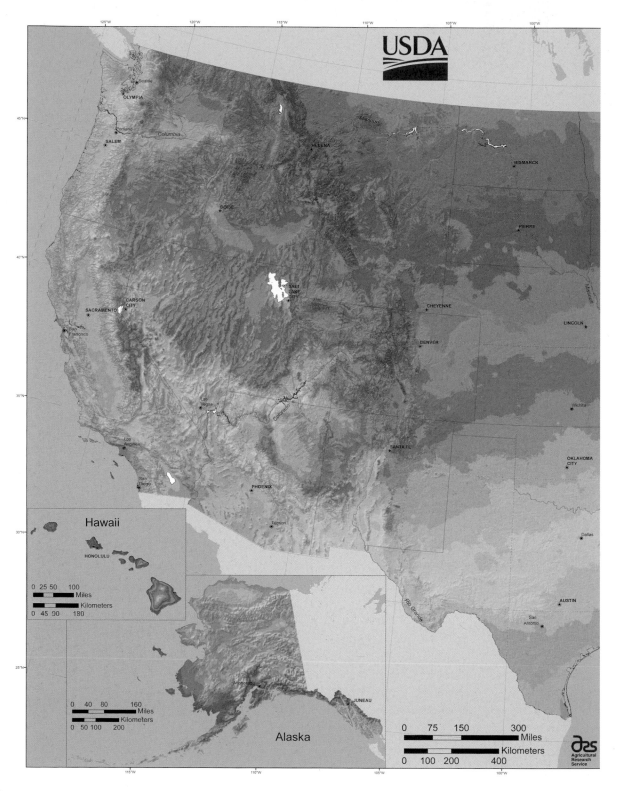

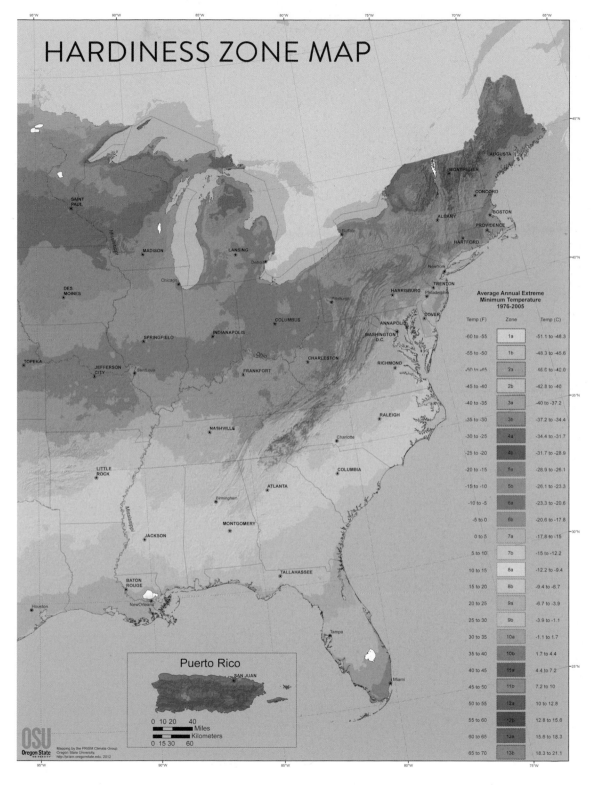

# HARDINESS ZONE MAP

### Average Annual Extreme Minimum Temperature 1976-2005

| Temp (F) | Zone | Temp (C) |
|---|---|---|
| -60 to -55 | 1a | -51.1 to -48.3 |
| -55 to -50 | 1b | -48.3 to -45.6 |
| -50 to -45 | 2a | -46.6 to -42.0 |
| -45 to -40 | 2b | -42.8 to -40 |
| -40 to -35 | 3a | -40 to -37.2 |
| -35 to -30 | 3b | -37.2 to -34.4 |
| -30 to -25 | 4a | -34.4 to -31.7 |
| -25 to -20 | 4b | -31.7 to -28.9 |
| -20 to -15 | 5a | -28.9 to -26.1 |
| -15 to -10 | 5b | -26.1 to -23.3 |
| -10 to -5 | 6a | -23.3 to -20.6 |
| -5 to 0 | 6b | -20.6 to -17.8 |
| 0 to 5 | 7a | -17.8 to -15 |
| 5 to 10 | 7b | -15 to -12.2 |
| 10 to 15 | 8a | -12.2 to -9.4 |
| 15 to 20 | 8b | -9.4 to -6.7 |
| 20 to 25 | 9a | -6.7 to -3.9 |
| 25 to 30 | 9b | -3.9 to -1.1 |
| 30 to 35 | 10a | -1.1 to 1.7 |
| 35 to 40 | 10b | 1.7 to 4.4 |
| 40 to 45 | 11a | 4.4 to 7.2 |
| 45 to 50 | 11b | 7.2 to 10 |
| 50 to 55 | 12a | 10 to 12.8 |
| 55 to 60 | 12b | 12.8 to 15.6 |
| 60 to 65 | 13a | 15.6 to 18.3 |
| 65 to 70 | 13b | 18.3 to 21.1 |

Puerto Rico

0 10 20 40
Miles
Kilometers
0 15 30 60

OSU
Oregon State
UNIVERSITY

Mapping by the PRISM Climate Group,
Oregon State University.
http://prism.oregonstate.edu, 2012

# PHOTOGRAPHY CREDITS

Helen Battersby: 215, 219, 224

Pam Beck: 220

Bluestone Perennials: 227, 228

Marguerite Brown: 44

Ciro Orabona Creative/Shutterstock.com: 52

islavicek/Shutterstock.com: 27

Janet Davis: 9 (right), 40, 51, 56, 80, 83, 95, 108, 204

Lynn Hunt: ii–iii, 19, 84, 120 (right), 139, 143, 211, 238

Lflorot/Shutterstock.com: 212

Betty Mackey: 103

M. J. McCabe: 184

Marush/Shutterstock.com: 123

Nancy J. Ondra:  i, iv–v, 3, 4, 5, 6 (top), 6 (bottom), 7, 8 (left and center),
9 (left and center), 11, 12, 15, 20, 24, 28, 31, 32, 39, 35, 43, 44,
47, 48, 55, 59, 64, 67, 68, 71, 72, 75, 76, 79, 87, 91, 92, 96, 99,
100, 104, 107, 111, 112, 114, 115 (top), 115 (bottom), 116, 117, 118, 119,
120 (left and center), 121 (all), 124, 127, 128, 131, 132, 135, 136, 140,
147, 148, 156, 160, 164, 167, 168, 172, 175, 176, 179, 183, 187, 188, 191,
192, 195, 196, 199, 200, 203, 207, 208, 216, 223, 230, 236

Rimashevskaya Olga/Shutterstock.com: 16

Manfred Ruckszio/Shutterstock.com: 152, 171

Carol Sandt: 88

Mark Turner: 180

Doreen Wynja: vi–1, 8 (right), 23, 60, 63, 144, 151, 155, 159, 163

COVER:

Background photo © Lukas Gojda / Shutterstock.com

Photos on left, from top to bottom: © Lynn Hunt, © Nancy J. Ondra,
© Nancy J. Ondra, © Doreen Wynja

# INDEX